HOW TO THRIVE
NOT JUST SURVIVE
THE
KINGDOM
WAY

MELANIE KOS-PAULA

Title: *How to Thrive*
Not Just Survive
the Kingdom Way!

Author: Melanie Kos-Paula
Copyright © 2015 Melanie Kos-Paula

Produced by: Galilee
www.galilee.nl
Cover/Interior design: Galilee

Royal Library The Netherlands registration number:
reg.nr: 020-14249
ISBN: 978-90-77607-75-6

FOREWORD

It is a great honor and privilege to be asked to write the Foreword for this book. Not only do I know Melanie well and appreciate how she lives what she writes, but also I realize God intended this book specifically for me.

Melanie is a master communicator. Her message is personal, simple, doable, and well-organized. As I began reading the pages of this book, I was immediately drawn in by Melanie's story and personal journey. She shares profound truths and gives practical ways to apply those to your life.

Melanie put it best when she wrote, "This book offers you simple yet profound insights and do-able steps. It is meant for believers desperately wanting to get out of their life of struggle. It is meant for those seeking a deeper walk with God. And it is also meant for non-believers trying to find out if God is real."

What jumped out the most for me was Melanie's statement that, "The key to steadily living a life of thriving is to first accept and believe the finished work of Christ. From that point on life is lived by putting God's truth above your circumstances, your feelings and your own knowledge of what you think is best, every day." If you are hungry for a breakthrough, meditate on that for a while.

Melanie also helps her reader to break down the internalized misconceptions that prevent us from realizing our true potential. This book will help you dismantle myths and overcome limiting beliefs. As you learn definite and clear distinctions between the kingdom of this world and the Kingdom of Heaven, you will be empowered to make better choices and experience more joy.

Moreover, Melanie includes "Focus points and tips for success" along with practical reflections at the end of each chapter. These tips enable the reader to become a stronger believer and "doer of the Word," as Melanie writes. If you have struggled believing in, and trusting in, a loving God, barriers will come down and relief will set in.

There are so many aspects of this book to enjoy such as the 'one problem-one focus' formula, dismantling two myths, getting to know the Father's love, and Practical 'Time-Tips'.

This book is packed full of pearls. It's easy to read and understand and will revolutionize your life if you apply its lessons. So find a comfortable place, start reading, and enjoy!

Blessings to thrive (not just survive) the Kingdom Way!

Joseph

Joseph Peck, M.D.
The Time Doctor
Author, I Was Busy Now I'm Not
www.empower2000.com

P.S. Let me leave you with this one final thought from How to Thrive: "Begin today to have the Word of God, the Bible, be your Absolute Guide and resolve never to step outside of it!"

Endorsements

"This book is simple to understand and well explained. Even a child can get it! It makes it easy to live the Christian life. It not only teaches you how to live the Christian life yourself, but also how to live with one another. It really brings everything about the Christian faith together. I immediately started putting the meditation exercises into practice. Fantastic!"

Maxine, reader

"Thanks to learning the definite and clear distinctions between the kingdom of this world and the Kingdom of Heaven, I have much less stress in my day. I can now more easily recognize, and subsequently follow the life I was meant to lead according to the Kingdom of Heaven. I also feel better equipped to reject that which is in discord with the Kingdom of Heaven and replace it with what God says is Truth."

Monique, reader

"I came from a religious and family background where guilt and self-condemnation were the ways to get me to live 'right'. I was often afraid to approach God after I had done something wrong because I learned that God would be mad at me. I had a dramatic shift of mind even after the very first chapters on 'My Truth'. I now understand that God is not mad at me. He loves me and wants me to come to Him even, and especially, when I fail. My prayer life is changing as I approach God the Father now with more confidence and an understanding that I am fully accepted by Him, no matter what! I am so thankful for this book. It is bringing me out of bondage!"

Cristina, reader

"My personal time with God was lacking. Now, I notice how differently my day goes when I put into practice what I learned in this book and devote the first few moments of the morning listening and receiving strength and direction from God. Since understanding the separation between the kingdom of this world and the Kingdom of Heaven it seems easier for me to step out of negative life patterns and find my way back to the attitudes and lifestyle God intended for me. My life will definitely be less complicated!"

Mattias, Reader

Dedication

I dedicate this book to my present day 'heroes of the faith' who have helped deepen my understanding of the "IT IS FINISHED" of Christ, and have given me the tools to daily live out my faith. You have opened my eyes to the truth that looking to the finished work of Christ is the only way to thrive!

To Pastor Joseph Prince, who taught me about God's unconditional love for me, no matter how often I fail or miss the mark.

To Pastor Dan Mohler, who taught me to never allow sin in others to produce sin in me.

To Pastor Tullian Tchividjian (Hope I got that last name right :-), who taught me to realize how desperately sinful my flesh is so that now I can truly appreciate God's amazing grace towards me.

To Pastor Jim Richards, who taught me how to persuade my heart to believe the truths of God's Word rather than the lies of my circumstances.

To Pastor Gary Keesee, who taught me how to get out from under the curse of toiling and begin living a life of tending in the garden of blessings God has provided for me.

I also dedicate this book to my life coach, Joseph Peck. You have taught me to hear God's voice and receive direction through lingering in His presence. Thank you for stretching me beyond my comfort zone and providing a safe launching pad from which to further step out into God's destiny and purpose for my life!

My life is forever changed!

Contents

Party 5: MY PURPOSE
Entering into My Destiny Freed from the Bondage of Toiling

Part 6: MY LIFESTYLE
Golden Nuggets for a Life of Success and Thriving

How to Thrive, (not Just Survive) *the Kingdom Way!*

Introduction

Are you struggling to merely get by in life? Are you living a defeated, unhappy and unfulfilled existence? Are your relationships failing? Are you living in a constant cycle of turmoil and stress, both personally and financially? Are you struggling to find stability and purpose? You don't need to anymore!

It is actually possible to thrive and not just survive, once you understand that you've been created for a life of fulfillment and limitlessness. There's no reason to stand on the sidelines and see others having their greatest desires fulfilled while you stand still and watch life pass you by. There's no reason to hope for the good things of life without ever seeing them come to pass. There's no reason to live by destructive and limiting beliefs that either you have set for your life or others have set for you. Neither is there reason to spend your life striving for provision and prosperity and miss out on fulfilling your God ordained purpose and destiny.

This book offers you simple yet profound insights and do-able steps. It is meant for believers desperately wanting to get out of their life of struggle. It is meant for those seeking a deeper walk with God. And it is also meant for non-believers trying to find out if God is real. The insights you will receive in this book will allow you to take hold of your life, creating and molding it into what it was made to be. Once understood and applied, you will clearly experience that a life of thriving is actually achievable for you! In this book I lay an unshakeable foundation. I paint a crystal clear picture of the path to a life of thriving that is open to you. There is a Kingdom way that will allow you to be stable and faith filled. You will know your identity and purpose and be well equipped to live life to its full potential!

Many have already gone before you and are experiencing profound growth in their lives by understanding and following what you will now learn. I myself experienced great development many years ago when I unknowingly began applying these principles to my own relationship struggles. The secret behind my past success, and the lessons I will teach you in this book, is the following: The key to steadily living a life of thriving is to first accept and believe the finished work of Christ. From that point on life is lived by putting God's truth above your circumstances, your feelings and your own knowledge of what you think is best, every day. At the base of this revelation is the understanding that this new way of life will be to your benefit and that of others, EVERY TIME. Why? Because it is based on a lifestyle of faith in the "It is finished" of Christ and subsequently on finding your identity in this finished work.

Since implementing these principles in my own life, I have been enjoying a fulfilling, abundant and uncomplicated existence. I only encounter struggle when I try tackling the issues of life myself, according to my own limited insight and knowledge. How silly to believe that my judgment is more valuable than God's! I have since been teaching people how to achieve this life and remain stable in their beliefs. Many are now seeing appreciable results as they learn to: 1. Focus on Christ; 2. Approach their life issues one at a time; and 3. Decide to first believe and then step out in the direction shown in God's Word. During this process they also learn to: 4. Remain focused on **the Kingdom truth about who they are, what they have, and what they can do**; and 5. Meditatively visualize their desired result before it actually occurs. Lives are forever transformed!

Now I know you might be saying: But I don't know anything about God's Word. I don't even go to church! How can I apply these principles to my life? If you don't know anything about God's Word, better for you! Why do I say that? Because you will have fewer misinterpretations of Bible truth to unlearn. It is sad to say this, but many who come from a church background have heard a lot of self-defeating and unbiblical teachings. Because of this they have a hard time accepting the beauty and simplicity of God's Word. So please, if you don't know God's Word yet, get to know Bible truths as presented in this book! I guarantee that you will see God in a way that you never have before.

Conversely, maybe you are saying: I've been to church before and I've read the Bible, but I don't believe in church or the Bible, because: "Look at all the horrible things those so-called Christian believers are doing to themselves and others. Why should I want what they say they believe? My answer to you is: "You just nailed it! **You don't need to live by what people SAY they believe!**" Get acquainted with the One who said it and then decide to get closer to Him, follow Him, and **BELIEVE what He says**, if you so desire. You may come to the sad realization that many who call themselves Christians are not at all living according to the directions of God's Word. Therefore, I want to gently encourage you who do not believe in church or the Bible as follows: Give yourself a fair chance to understand what the Word of God is really about and what it can mean for you. After that, if you want to follow, then follow. Deal? Let's step into this together!

For those of you more adamant in your dislike of God, this book was also written with you in mind. Maybe you are saying to yourself: "I hate God!" or: "In my world, God doesn't exist. I have not taken the time or made the effort to read the Bible or attend any church. Because, how can there be a God when there's so much junk and pain going on in the world? What kind of God just watches this all happen and does absolutely nothing to stop the pain, the suffering and violence? Don't you Christians say that He claims to have the power to do anything?" To you I say: "please bear with me". Let's go through this book together. It could possibly make a difference for you when you understand God's true intention for the world and for all mankind. I extend to you the invitation to walk through the pages of this book with me. In the end, if your view is still the same, set aside everything you've read and continue on your journey. I then thank you and commend you for having given me and my message the value of your time. But if you have a change of mind about who God is and what His plans and intentions are for mankind, then please promise to drop me a line and let me know about it, okay?

The truth is that many of us believers have not done a very good job of showing life as God intended it. As a result, non-believers and non-churchgoers have seldom seen the Kingdom of Heaven truly reflected. Yet, no matter what your challenges in life, you can share the experience of many by beginning to see your life transform, after reading even only the first few pages of this book.

You too will quickly discover that the key to thriving in life is to:1. **Discover that your true identity has been restored back to you by Jesus' finished work through the shedding of His blood; 2. Boldly accept your restored Godly identity; 3. Re-program the destructive and limiting beliefs of your**

heart conforming them to your new identity; 4. Live from your new Godly identity; and 5. Be all that God says you are, have all that God says is yours, and do all that God says you can! The secret to your success in life is centered around your willingness to live by what God says is true about you. From this point on you no longer focus on man's opinions or on negative circumstances. You also do not focus anymore on the lies you have believed about yourself, your qualities and your purpose.

This book consists of six parts. In each one, I seek to persuade you to see Christ. I then gently lead you to use His lenses (so to speak) to see who you are, what you have and what you can do according to the Kingdom of Heaven. I also offer strategies to help you shake off your earthly limitations and step into the glory of what Christ accomplished for you at the cross. Here's an overview of what you will learn in this book and how people's lives are already being changed by it.

- Part 1: 'My Beginning', describes my personal path in the area of learning to thrive rather than just survive in life. It tells of how my life began to radically improve once I began walking out my God-given identity. Those who made the first part of this journey with me were inspired by my personal story, and you can read more about my struggles and victories in my book titled: *My Husband, My Lord, My All.* [1]

- Part 2: 'My Truth', deals with the importance of having a correct understanding of Bible truths. It gives a clear account of why the person Jesus Christ is so essential in the life of the believer, and what this means for their own sense of self. People have been profoundly impacted as they found out about their new identity through the finished work of

Christ. As a result, they have renewed their mind to the Kingdom of Heaven and immediately began experiencing Kingdom blessings, firsthand.

- Part 3: 'My Faith', teaches the true meaning of believing in God's Word and His promises. I talk about how biblical meditation helps replace destructive heart beliefs back to the truths of the Kingdom of Heaven. Those who have learned to activate their faith in this way are now experiencing Bible faith as the key to bringing Kingdom reality into their life.

- Part 4: 'My Identity', gets into who God has called us to be and how to use forgiveness to free ourselves from destructive and limiting beliefs. Many have flourished once they stopped defining their lives by negative circumstances and the opinions of man. Instead, they allowed God to completely define their identity.

- Part 5: 'My Purpose', teaches you how acquiring provision the Kingdom Way sets you free to pursue your God-given purpose in life. Once you have adopted these principles into your life, you too will join the many others who no longer have to struggle for provision according to worldly standards.

- And finally, Part 6: 'My Lifestyle', teaches you to take responsibility for your own success in life. Here you learn to eliminate time-wasters and create your own personal vision board to see the life you want, right in front of you! Developing a Kingdom lifestyle by maintaining high personal standards has led to ongoing peace and victory for many.

I promise you that the people who have experienced victory by applying what this book has to offer, are the rule, and not the exceptions. This could be your experience, too! So please read on to learn how the finished work of Christ allows you to embrace your true identity, empowering you to thrive and not just survive, the Kingdom Way!

Some final notes from the author
About the Bible verses used in this book
The cited Bible verses are taken from both the King James Version (KJV)[2] and the New International Version (NIV).[3] These sources were chosen based on their relevance to the text.

The 'one problem-one focus' formula
Before plunging into the content, I would like to suggest the most effective way of working through the pages of this book. I realize that you may be struggling in several areas of your life. Still, right now, I invite you to please choose one specific life situation that you would like to change. Write it down. As you read, take time to refer to the 'focus points and tips for success' and 'practical reflection and consideration' sections at the end of each chapter. Then evaluate your result at the end of the book. Will you do that? Alright, then let's get started!

PART 1
THE BEGINNING
The Struggles That Led to a New Way of Life

Chapter 1
How It All Began

Many years ago I went through a rough period in my life. I found myself having to deal with betrayal and divorce. I was forced to come to terms with the fact that life could suddenly and unexpectedly change. Once it did, I had no choice but to come to terms with who I really am and for what I stand. At that time, everything in my life came crashing down. I was taken completely off guard and had many questions and doubts in my mind. How could this have happened? Where did things go wrong? How could I make it better again?

I soon learned what was at the basis of my personal failures and mistakes in my marriage. Throughout my elementary school years I struggled with a low sense of self-worth and an inability to express my true feelings. This often resulted in fits of anger and periods of heavy migraine attacks and depression. It also ultimately led to my divorce.

For a long time I struggled to 'let go of a dead thing'. My relationship was over, yet I strained for many months to try and pick up from where I left off. In doing so I always met with rejection and further alienation from the one with whom I once so closely shared my life. As I stubbornly continued trying to glue the broken pieces together, my heart felt like it was on an emotional roller coaster. As I embarked on the tumultuous journey, I felt split in two. On the one hand I wanted to make amends. Yet, at the same time I wanted to call it quits, pick up the broken pieces and try to get my life back together again. Because of all the hardships I was facing, a friend invited me to move to Holland for a temporary break from my circumstances. This is how I left my birth island Curaçao to start a new life in Holland, far away from home.

The first part of my time in Holland was complicated and felt desolate. Once I had decided to remain in Holland for a longer period, I was in dire financial need. I didn't even have money to pay for bus fare to go to my job interviews or to make a phone call to my parents whom I had left behind in Curaçao. This became a time of buckling up and making a decision as to which way I wanted to go with my life and how to make it happen.

Yet as if that was not enough, I also had to come to terms with my abortion that I had committed years earlier. I went through a period of harsh attacks of guilt and self-condemnation for past mistakes in my life. Desperation and the lies of the enemy overtook me and convinced me that I did not deserve anything good from God anymore.

Nevertheless, early on in the struggle I sensed that something good would come out of it all. Though on the one hand my heart was bleeding, there was also a calmness that convinced me that all was well. My inner compass helped me stay on course, continuously looking out for the good that was in store for me. So, despite the reality of pain and confusion, my spirit proved more than able to cope.

I determined to keep a positive attitude and include God in the process of revealing to me my mistakes and shortcomings. I developed a lifestyle of continual prayer and close communion with Holy Spirit and made good use of my time alone. I worshipped and got to know God better each day. I had no greater desire than to live for God and obey Him in all that He asked of me. My intimate relationship with Papa (Father God), Jesus and Holy Spirit made me see many of my prayers answered quickly and in extraordinary ways. I soon discovered that confessing the Word (saying what God says) was a powerful weapon against any feelings of defeat and desperation I faced. I accepted God's unconditional love for me and allowed His Word to speak louder than my circumstances and feelings. Every time I did this I was lifted out of my situation of despair and defeat, without fail.

I did not realize at the time what I was doing, but later came to understand that I was 'choosing the Kingdom Way above the way of this world'. I began believing and using God's Word as a tool to break through my circumstances and feelings. This became my first step in seeing my life transform and transcend above and beyond what I could have ever imagined. I began to see that I had found the key to breakthrough in every area of my life. Sometimes when my flesh wanted to retaliate and choose 'the way that seems right to man', there was a struggle. But I learned more and more to choose the Kingdom Way over my own and saw the benefits of The Kingdom of Heaven manifest in my life!

In the years that followed up until today, I have continued building on the foundation of The Kingdom of Heaven. I have since understood the true value of living according to my God-given identity based on the finished work of Christ. I have learned to boldly step into the life of blessings that He so lovingly provided. The teachings in this book are based on many years of my personal experience, many years of hours spent studying God's Word, and many years of learning from great men of God. To this day, their teachings and sermons continue to help me further develop who I am in God. My personal life and my outlook on life have dramatically changed since I began learning and applying the principles I will teach you in this book.

So right now I encourage you to throw every limitation out the window. Every voice that may be telling you that this has worked for others but that it will not work for you. Throw out every lie that says that the effects of your past cannot be healed or that your Bible knowledge is not enough to make it through life and thrive as you go. I am offering you a new way to live! Read on to learn how starting today you can thrive and not just survive in your personal life - the Kingdom Way!

PART 2
MY TRUTH
Establishing a Firm Foundation in Kingdom Principles

CHAPTER 2
The Importance of Right Believing

Purpose: In this chapter you will learn why it is important to have a correct understanding cf Bible truths and biblical terms.

I want to first begin by asking a few simple yet defining questions. Let's get started right away: First of all, are you reading the Word of God, the Bible, but not knowing how to apply the truths written in it? Have you stopped reading the Bible altogether because you don't understand and can't make sense of what it says? Are you wondering what to make of God as you read the Word? Are you asking yourself things like: "Is He a good God or a bad God? Is this passage of scripture applicable to me or is it not? Do I need to follow Old Testament or New Testament Laws?"

If you answered yes to any of the questions above, have you decided to just try to make the best of life on your own? Have you decided to struggle along and just see where things will end up for you? Then I promise you, this chapter and the next will give you the answers and the tools to get a clear understanding of how to relate to Bible Truth in a practical and personal way. You will learn to make the Word of God applicable in your daily life.

Dismantling two myths:

Before going on I want to dismantle two myths. Why? Because they have made children of God get into trouble with their faith. They have hindered many who genuinely want to live the Christian life in their ability to trust God.

The first myth that needs to be torn down is this one: "God sends trials to test me". The Bible clearly states that God tests no man and that He is even unable to do so, because all that comes from Him is only good, and He does not waiver in this. *When tempted, no one should say, "God is tempting me." For God cannot be tempted by evil, nor does he tempt anyone; but each person is tempted when they are dragged away by their own evil desire and enticed. Then, after desire has conceived, it gives birth to sin; and sin, when it is full-grown, gives birth to death. Don't be deceived, my dear brothers and sisters. Every good and perfect gift is from above, coming down from the Father of the heavenly lights, who does not change like shifting shadows (Jas. 1:13-17).*

As long as we still believe that God sends evil upon us to teach us some deep life lesson, we will never be able to fully trust Him. How can we? If the One who is supposed to help us is also the one sending the trouble, how will we judge His dependability when we are going through hard times? So please decide right now to throw this lie out the window!

The second myth, while seeming contradictory to the first, is also based on false pretenses that must be abandoned in order to build a trusting relationship with God. Myth number 2: "Having faith in God, through Jesus Christ is supposed to give me a 'good life' on earth". We must reject this myth because of the superficiality that it implies. Jesus was not sent to suffer and die to give us a 'good life'. His purpose was to restore us back to the original position of Sonship, the identity and purpose we had with God before sin entered into the world. He came to restore us back to who we were created to be. What He promised us was not a 'good life', but rather an <u>abundant LIFE</u>. This abundant life exchanges all that the devil has brought through sin with blessings for us who believe. *The thief comes only to steal and kill and destroy; I came that they may have life, and have it abundantly (John 10:10).* This means that even in the midst of trials, tribulations, and hardships on the journey of life, we radiate His love, peace, dominion, joy, compassion, and abundant provision.

Even through hardships we are able to manifest His Godly character and remain stable and Christ-like. Jesus' coming was never about us running after the 'good things' of life. What we run after and pursue is getting to know Him, the Giver of this abundant life. From that close relationship we re-discover ourselves and find out who we are really meant to be. That's what this life is all about! The quality of that life grows as we get to know Father God, Jesus and Holy Spirit more intimately each day! The 'good things' then automatically follow.

How to relate to Bible truth
Without getting into too much detail, here are some practical points to consider as you read the Word of God:

1. When you read the Old Testament realize that we struggle today with the same issues as the Israelites did in those days. We are all sinful by nature because of the fall of man. We, on our own, are incapable of adhering to God's holy standard for life. *For all have sinned and fall short of the glory of God (Rom. 3:23).* For the Israelites this meant that a priest had to regularly make sacrifices to atone for their sins. In spite of this they never

became righteous (as they should be) in God's eyes. In the New Testament there is a difference. Christ has offered Himself as the ultimate sacrifice for all of our sins. By going to the cross and shedding His blood, we have been redeemed in the eyes of God. All men are now righteous through their faith. As the Bible says: *Even the righteousness of God through faith in Jesus Christ for all those who believe; for there is no distinction (Rom. 3:22).*

Our position of righteousness allows us, as children of God to now partake of every blessing and promise God made in His Word. *For by these He has granted to us His precious and magnificent promises, so that by them you may become partakers of the divine nature, having escaped the corruption that is in the world by lust (2 Pet. 1:4).*

If you are a believer, all the promises God ever made in both the Old Testament and the New Testament are for you and to you. Every promise once spoken by God stands for **all times, for all people**. The Bible teaches that: *For no matter how many promises God has made, they are "Yes" in Christ. And so through him the "Amen" is spoken by us to the glory of God (2 Corinthians 1:20).*

2. The Ten Commandments given to the Israelites through Moses were intended to make them realize their inability to uphold God's high standard of holiness and, thus, their need for a Savior. God's high standard of holiness still applies today, but the Savior we needed was Jesus who came to do for us what we could never do for ourselves. He kept every commandment and fulfilled every law, living a holy and sinless life. He did this out of love on our behalf. *He who knew no sin became sin for us so that we would be brought back into fellowship with God. God made him who had no sin to be sin for us, so that in him we might become the righteousness of God (2 Corinthians 5:21). And He Himself bore our sins in His body on the cross, so that we might*

die to sin and live to righteousness; for by His wounds you were healed (1 Pet. 2:24). Jesus paid our penalty for sin by dying for us. Then He rose again and took every believer with Him in His victory over sin. Now when God looks at us He sees us as if we have never sinned, leading lives of righteousness. *When you were dead in your transgressions and the uncircumcision of your flesh, He made you alive together with Him, having forgiven us all our transgressions (Col. 2:13).*

3. In the Old Testament, especially in the Psalms, you find words like: *O LORD, why do You reject my soul? Why do You hide Your face from me? (Ps. 88:14). Your furious anger crushes me (Ps. 88:16).* When you read these type of passages, realize that 2000 years ago, as Jesus took His place on the cross to absolve for your sins, God rejected Jesus, crushed Jesus and turned His face away from Jesus. Thanks to Jesus' sacrifice, God will never reject you or turn away from you again. Ever! Jesus Christ paid the price for you!

So, now you can read those same words and say: "Thank you, Lord that you will never reject me. Your face will never again be turned away from me, and You will always look upon me with love".

4. The Old Testament mentions words like: *I long to be in Your temple (Ps. 84:2)* or *We are going into the house of God to worship Him (Ps. 122:1).* When you read this, realize that we don't need to go anywhere to find and worship God anymore. In Christ, He now permanently lives in our heart. We have now become the temple within which He dwells.

Everything has already been fulfilled and made 'present tense' for us in Christ. So whenever the Old Testament refers to blessings that **will be** yours in the future, read it all in the present tense, because all of it has already been given to you when Christ gave His life for you at the cross! All you now have to do is to believe!

In fact, be aware that we no longer need to pursue anything that the Old Testament people did to try to please God. He already is pleased with us because of our acceptance of His Son's sacrifice on or behalf. He made us accepted in the beloved (Eph. 1:6).

5. When you read the gospels (Matthew, Mark, Luke and John) do not identify yourself with the pharisees, nor with the ooh-ing and aah-ing crowds, and not even with the disciples. Because of Christ's work of eternal salvation for us we only identify ourselves with, and place ourselves in, Christ alone. That is how God sees you. He is who you're called to be like in every way - being who He was, doing what He did and having what He had. *"Truly, truly, I say to you, he who believes in Me, the works that I do, he will do also; and greater works than these he will do; because I go to the Father" (John 14:12). By this, love is perfected with us, so that we may have confidence in the day of judgment; because as He is, so also are we in this world (1 John 4:17).* You must no longer strive for perfection because Christ has achieved perfection for you, even when you fail. This certainly does give a whole different perspective on life...

6. Be sure to always correctly divide the Word of God. Find out if the portion of scripture is written to the Jews or the gentiles (you). If it is written to the Jews, learn from what is said, but don't try to put yourself under the yoke of trying to live it. *It is for freedom that Christ has set us free. Stand firm, then, and do not let yourselves be burdened again by a yoke of slavery (Gal. 5:1).* You are called to be free in Christ who has already fulfilled every law by living a sinless life. You are now called righteous because of faith in Him.

The books Galatians, Ephesians, Philippians and Colossians give an especially clear view of the life and position of the believer in Christ today, a life of faith and acceptance of all that Christ has accomplished for us through His blood and the cross.

I hope the above serves you in better understanding the Word of God, and I hope these practical tips will allow you to begin to see God's goodness and His loving kindness toward you in a whole new way. The rest of this book will hopefully give you an even better understanding of God and His Word.

The meaning of some important words:
I now want to show you the meaning of some important words used in the Bible. These words will be referenced several times throughout this book. Here they are:

Repent   : to change your mind
Righteous : I am as I should be
Grace   : ability, unmerited favor
Salvation : saved (from hell to heaven), but also: healed, delivered, prosperous, whole, protected, provided for
Peace   : nothing missing, nothing broken
Sin   : to miss the mark
Blessed   : set apart, taken from the realm of the Kingdom of this world (the earth-cursed system) and placed under the authority of The Kingdom of Heaven.

I believe it is critical to know the true meaning of words because, only then can their power be truly manifested as an agent of change in your life. Understanding these words alone, will bring more depth to your Bible reading experience.

In the next chapter I will take you on a journey through the Bible. I will mark **four prominent events** that are crucial for understanding the essence of how to thrive, and not just survive, the Kingdom way!

Focus points and tips for success on my journey to personal thriving, the Kingdom Way:

- I decide today to believe that trials are never from God.
- I will actively discern which portions of the Bible are written to me and allow only those passages to shape Godly character in me.

Practical reflection and consideration ('My Truth'):

Have you been deceived by any of these myths? How do you feel now that they have been dismantled?

By doing this exercise I learned about myself that:

_____

_____

_____

_____

_____

_____

_____

_____

_____

_____

_____

_____

_____

_____

_____

_____

_____

_____

_____

CHAPTER 3
General Overview of Four Main Events

Purpose: In this chapter you will learn Bible truths that will help you understand why Christ's coming into this world is so crucial to the life of the believer.

I will be taking you through the stories of Adam and Eve, Abraham and Sarah, Moses and finally Jesus Christ, our Lord and Savior. Let's begin!

1. Adam and Eve: Before and after the fall. Key word: THE CURSE
Some passages to study about Adam and Jesus
Adam: Son of God (Luke 3:38), First Adam (1 Cor. 15:44,) Earthly/fleshly (1 Cor. 15:47), Living soul (1 Cor. 15:45).
Jesus: Son of God (John 17:1, Luke 3:21-22), Last Adam (1 Cor. 15:45), From heaven (1 Cor. 15:47), Life-giving Spirit (1 Cor. 15:45).

As we look at the life of Adam and Eve in the garden of Eden I will use key points to describe the events that occurred before and after the fall. After that I will give a short explanation of what actually went on at that time.

Before the fall:
Adam was called Son of God (Luke 3:38)
Adam was created in the image and likeness of God (Gen. 1:26)
There was spiritual life (Gen. 2:7)
There was blessing (Gen. 1:28)
Man was called to subdue and reign on the earth (Gen. 1:28)
Man was planted and placed by God in an environment where there were crops and abundant provision (Gen. 2:8-10)
Man only had to tend and take care of the garden (Gen. 2:15)
Man enjoyed communion with God, with each other, and with nature (Gen. 2:15-23)
Man lived with God inside the garden and had complete trust in Him (Gen. 2:8-25)

After the fall:
Man was referred to as "Sons of the devil" (John 8:44)
Man was referred to as "made in the image of the fallen Adam" (Gen. 5:3)
There was spiritual death (Gen. 2:16-17)
The earth became cursed (Gen. 3:14-17)
Man lost his position of reigning and dominion (Gen. 3:17-19)
Man had to painfully toil to gather provision in an earth-cursed environment (Gen. 3:17)
Man ate by the sweat of his brow (Gen. 3:19)
Man lived in fear, shame, and enmity with God and with each other (Gen. 3:10-13)
Man lived without God outside the garden and began to trust in himself (Gen. 3:23)

I want to encourage you to read the entire account of Adam and Eve for yourself. When you do, you will notice that there was absolutely no dissonance between man and God before sin came into the world. Man never struggled to adhere to the high and pure standard of God, because he was created in God's image and likeness. Man never wondered if what he was doing was right or wrong, because he lived 'in God', in oneness, and communion with Him, having no consciousness of sin. Therefore man continued as God is.

Man never knew stress and toiling for provision because all man was intended to do was to tend the earth. His only assignment was to maintain the perfect state in which it was originally created. Man never knew fear, because he lived in the perfect love of God where no fear existed. Man never had to ask for anything, because all he needed was already there for the taking. Picture all this and realize: This is your life! This is your identity! This is who you were called to be before sin came in and messed up everything. Do you understand this? Do you see the difference between the life we were called to and the life many of us are actually living? That, "before-the-fall-life" belongs to you today, right now!

Man never knew evil, because it did not play a role until man handed his God-given dominion over to the devil. From the moment man ate from the tree of the knowledge of good and evil from which God had said, "Do not eat", everything changed. The world was no longer ruled and governed by the perfect, peaceful, and harmonious will of a loving God. **Man let go of the truth that he already was completely 'as God' and in that instant handed over his dominion, provision, health, peace, and everything else that belonged to his true nature and identity to the devil.** The earth curse was now a fact: Man was taken over and shaped by the sinful nature and character of the devil. A curse of evil spread over the once perfect earth, leading to a pandemic of murder, lying, deception, enmity, rape, sickness, depression, perversion, selfishness, need, etc.

Now man, rather than talking and listening to God, began listening to the devil and to his own reasoning and interpretations about right and wrong. Man based his life on his own five senses, which were by now completely corrupted by evil. From that point on the life of sin became a reality. A life that was never intended by God. Never! But thankfully, our loving God had a perfect plan in place that would offer us a way back to His original intention for us. Please continue reading to understand more about God's plan of restoration and bringing you back to your original identity in Him and with Him.

Let's now look at the life of Abram (Abraham) and Sarai (Sarah)
2. Abram and Sarai: One life, one promise. Key Word: RIGHTEOUSNESS
Some passages to study about Abraham and Jesus:
Abraham: Father of us all through life of faith (Rom. 4:16, Gal. 3:6), Promises spoken to Abraham and his seed (Gal. 3:16).
Jesus: Son of Abraham (Matt. 1:1), Christ is the seed (Gal. 3:16).

Abram and Sarai lived in the earth-cursed system, yet there was something significantly different about their lives. Abram was not a perfect man. This is evident from the fact that he, on two occasions, told his wife to lie to the rulers of the country. She was to say that she was Abram's sister. The reason for this was because Sarai was so beautiful, Abram was afraid that the rulers would kill him so that they could take Sarai as their own. In spite of telling lies, which was a consequence of the earth curse, Abram was abundantly blessed by these same rulers, even as they found out about his deceit. The Bible says that Pharaoh, and not Abram (!), was punished for Abram's acts.

After being found out, Abram was sent away with a rich provision of Pharaoh's cattle, servants and camels. The rulers willingly left Abram with all they had given him, just to get him, whom God considered righteous, out of their sight! *'And when Pharaoh's officials saw her, they praised her to Pharaoh, and she was taken into his palace. He treated Abram well for her sake, and Abram acquired sheep and cattle, male and female donkeys, male and female servants, and camels. But the LORD inflicted serious diseases on Pharaoh and his household because of Abram's wife Sarai. So Pharaoh summoned Abram. "What have you done to me?" he said. "Why didn't you tell me she was your wife? Why did you say, 'She is my sister,' so that I took her to be my wife? Now then, here is your wife. Take her and go!" Then Pharaoh gave orders about Abram to his men, and they sent him on his way, with his wife and everything he had (Gen. 12:15-20).*

The life of Sarai was also characterized by wrong decisions, jealousy, faultfinding and strife - all consequences of the earth curse (Gen. 16:1-5, Gen. 21:10). Yet she was also blessed beyond measure and became the bearer of Isaac, the promised son through whom the whole earth would be blessed. God then changed their names to Abraham and Sarah.

How could this be? Why weren't Abraham and Sarah punished for their ungodliness (Gen. 12:11-16)? How could their living outside of God's framework be without consequence for them? It is because God chose to make a covenant with Abraham. A covenant that was not built upon upholding the law and perfectly living up to God's standards, but upon **righteousness by faith** (Gen. 22:15-18, Rom. 4:3-4).

God decided to choose Abraham as a vessel through which He would point to the finished work that Jesus would one day do for us at the cross. The finished work that would cause us to be called 'righteous by faith'. The finished work that would have nothing to do with our own righteousness, but would be solely dependent upon Christ's righteousness on our behalf. We are called righteous because we believe in the sacrifice of the righteous One, Jesus Christ!

Pointing to the future - parallel truth between Abraham and Jesus

Let's look at some examples of how Abraham's life parallels truths in the New Testament. I invite you to please look up the following verses for yourself. Abraham was told that his descendants would be *strangers in a land not their own* (Gen. 15:13). This points to the New Covenant believers in relation to the Kingdom of Heaven, for the Bible says that believers are *citizens of the Kingdom of Heaven*, thus having become strangers on this earth (Phil. 3:20).

God also refers to the promises as being spoken to both Abraham and his seed, Christ (Gal. 3:16). God made an *eternal Covenant with Abraham* (Gen. 17:3-8), just as *Jesus made with us through His finished work on the cross* (Heb. 13:20). The promises made are those of *abundant blessing for Abraham and his descendants* (Gen. 22:17-18, John 10:10). One of these promises was that *Abraham would reign and rule over his enemies* (Gen. 22-17) and take possession of the earth just as *we would again reign over the devil* under the New Covenant, (Matt. 16:18-19).

As Abraham became a vessel for God's promises, blessings once again took the place of curses. This happened not because Abraham did everything right, but because he trusted the promises/the Word of God in spite of his own feelings and personal reasoning. We see a clear example of this when God told Abraham to sacrifice his only son, Isaac on the altar. Abraham walked up the mountain with Isaac to be sacrificed, while Isaac carried the wood on his back the whole way. Then God said, *"Take your son, your only son, whom you love—Isaac—and go to the region of Moriah. Sacrifice him there as a burnt offering on a mountain I will show you." Early the next morning Abraham got up and loaded his donkey. He took with him two of his servants and his son Isaac. When he had cut enough wood for the burnt offering, he set out for the place God had told him about.*

On the third day Abraham looked up and saw the place in the distance. He said to his servants, "Stay here with the donkey while I and the boy go over there. We will worship and then we will come back to you." Abraham took the wood for the burnt offering and placed it on his son Isaac, and he himself carried the fire and the knife. As the two of them went on together, Isaac spoke up and said to his father Abraham, "Father?" "Yes, my son?" Abraham replied "The fire and wood are here," Isaac said, "but where is the lamb for the burnt offering?" Abraham answered, "God himself will provide the lamb for the burnt offering, my son." And the two of them went on together (Gen. 22:2-3). Abraham's act of faith on the mountain perfectly parallels the act of God with His son Jesus. Just like Isaac, Jesus carried the wooden cross on His back as He went up the mountain of Calvary. There He would be sacrificed at the cross once and for all for the sins of all humanity.

God used Abraham as a messenger for the truth that one day Father God would knowingly and willingly deliver up His Son for us. God reinstated man to his original created value when Jesus became the ultimate sacrifice for us. We can now live once again having communion with God and living by His spoken word. We no longer need to depend on our own limited reasoning and senses.

In this example it is evident that according to the Bible, faith and obedience go hand in hand! Abraham did not stop to reason about what would happen if Isaac, his child of the promise, would die at the altar. He heard God's Word and promptly chose to obey (Gen. 22:8). This is to be the mark of every believer who lives under the New Covenant of the finished work of Christ!

3. MOSES. The ten commandments and the altar. Key word: CONDEMNATION

Some passages to study about Moses and Jesus

Moses: The law came through Moses (John 1:17), the blood of bulls and goats, sacrifices (Heb. 10:4), the Old Covenant, unable to save (Rom. 8:3), the Sabbath rest (Deut. 5:12-15).

Jesus: Grace and truth came through Jesus (John 1:17), the blood of Jesus, once and for all sacrifice (Heb. 9:28), the New Covenant, salvation in Christ (Rom. 8:3), 'Today' is the day of rest in Christ (Heb. 4:1-11).

As time progressed, sin continued to be rampant in the world. People were unable to keep the holy standards of God, instead creating their own standards by which to live, judging right and wrong according to their own criterion. It was at this time that God raised up Moses giving him the Ten Commandments and the mandate to build an altar of sacrifice (Exod. 20:1-17, 24).

What was the significance of the Ten Commandments and the altar? The Bible teaches us that the purpose of the law (the Ten Commandments) was to make sin 'show-up'. *Why, then, was the law given at all? It was added because of transgressions until the Seed to whom the promise referred had come (Gal. 3:19).*

Let me explain by way of an example. If a street has no traffic lights, you can drive up and down that street and decide for yourself when to stop and when to go. You can also decide never to stop if you don't feel like it. In both cases you have done nothing wrong. You drive and trust your own ability and insight, using your five senses (again, which have been corrupted by sin) to decide when to drive and when to stop.

However, once the law enforcers decide to put traffic lights on that same street, everything changes. Once they explain to you the meaning of the red, orange, and green lights, you KNOW that you have violated a law when you drive through the red light. So, once the light exists and you understand its meaning you can then become aware of your offense. The same was the purpose of the Ten Commandments.

Until the time of the Ten Commandments people were erroneously convinced that they could do everything the Lord expected of them. They had absolutely no idea how far sin had taken them away from the high and holy standard of God. Yet, it was just a few short days after the Ten Commandments were given to Moses, that they proved their inability to do what God asked of them. They broke one of the very first commandments which read: *'You shall not make for yourself an image in the form of anything in heaven above or on the earth beneath or in the waters below. You shall not bow down to them or worship them' (Exod. 20:3-5).* But, what did they do? They made a golden calf and called it their God. *When the people saw that Moses was so long in coming down from the mountain, they gathered around Aaron and said, "Come, make us gods who will go before us. As for this fellow Moses who brought us up out of Egypt, we don't know what has happened to him."*

Aaron answered them, "Take off the gold earrings that your wives, your sons and your daughters are wearing, and bring them to me." So all the people took off their earrings and brought them to Aaron. He took what they handed him and made it into an idol cast in the shape of a calf, fashioning it with a tool. Then they said, "These are your gods, Israel, who brought you up out of Egypt."

When Aaron saw this, he built an altar in front of the calf and announced, "Tomorrow there will be a festival to the LORD." So the next day the people rose early and sacrificed burnt offerings and presented fellowship offerings. Afterward they sat down to eat and drink and got up to indulge in revelry.

Then the LORD said to Moses, "Go down, because your people, whom you brought up out of Egypt, have become corrupt. They have been quick to turn away from what I commanded them and have made themselves an idol cast in the shape of a calf. They have bowed down to it and sacrificed to it and have said, 'These are your gods, Israel, who brought you up out of Egypt (Exod. 32:1-8).

In His merciful compassion God chose to provide a temporary way out for those who broke His holy standard. Right after Moses received the Ten Commandments, God told him to build an altar of sacrifice. At this altar priests would continually make animal sacrifices, shedding the blood of blameless animals to atone for the sins of the people. When the sacrifice was made, the priest laid his hand on the head of both the animal and the sinner. This act depicted the transfer of man's sin into the blameless animal, and that of the innocent animal into the sinner. After the sacrifice the sinner would walk away free as if he had never sinned, while the innocent animal was slain and burnt outside the camp.

This sacrifice was enacted many years later in all its fullness. Jesus, who is called the lamb of God who knew no sin, became our replacement by the shedding of His blood. There He took our sins upon Himself, once and for all. Because of His sacrifice we could walk away free from the burden of sin, as if we never did anything wrong. From that moment we were considered righteous once we put our faith in Him! (Lev. 4:13-21, Heb. 13:12). Do you see how all this is coming together?

It is interesting to note that in the time of Moses a distinction was made between conscious sin and sin done in ignorance. Conscious sin was immediately punished by death (Deut. 22:20-24, Exod. 21:12,15,17, Lev. 20:9-16), while the altar of sacrifice was put into place for sins done in ignorance. Yet the Bible teaches that Jesus in His awesome mercy and love for us, bore both our sins done in ignorance (iniquities) and our conscious sins (transgressions), when He shed His blood for our atonement. But He was pierced through for our transgressions,

He was crushed for our iniquities (Isa. 53:5). Hallelujah, Thank you Lord for such a complete salvation!

The Ten Commandments were God's way of showing man his incapability of fully obeying Him. It was proof that God's holy standard and perfection were too high for sinful man to attain by his own effort. The Ten Commandments also proved man's need for a Savior. Because the standard of God was unattainable, someone was needed who could live the sinless, perfect life for us. Someone was needed to remove every lowly, earthly curse of sin that stuck to man since the fall. We needed someone who would forgive us completely and fully - one who by His holiness and sacrifice would restore us back to the high standard we enjoyed with God before sin and the earth-curse entered the world.

The choice is yours
We learn from the story in the garden of Eden that God did not intervene and try to stop Adam and Eve from eating from the tree. Once He had spoken His Word: *You shall not eat from the tree...* God left the choice either to obey or disobey entirely up to Adam and Eve. God in His sovereign love will never force man to do His will. He wants His children to obey Him out of love, not coercion or fear of punishment. The choice to accept or reject Jesus as Savior is also entirely up to you. God has already made the provision for us through Christ. Accepting Him will bring you into a relationship with God like Adam had before the earth became cursed.

Allowing Christ to enter your life will enable all of God's blessings to follow. The life of Abraham gives us a clear picture of how this relationship looks for the believer in the midst of the earth-cursed system: In God's eyes you are considered righteous by faith in Him instead of righteous by your works. With that, you receive every blessing you had in God before the fall.

Rejection of the Savior would mean a life of continued strife. You will always be trying in your own strength and by your own limited (fallen) means to attain those things that have already been freely given to you by Christ's sacrifice. Rejection of the Savior will also mean that you choose to carry the weight and burden of trying to make it in the earth-cursed system by yourself. But listen: You don't have to. You now have a choice!

There are some who erroneously believe and teach that unless you accept Jesus Christ as your Savior, God will not love you. This is a lie! God has already proven His love for you by sending His son to suffer and die for you at the cross, even long before you ever knew about Him or wanted to have anything to do with Him. *But God demonstrates His own love toward us, in that while we were yet sinners, Christ died for us* (Rom. 5:8). It is not God's love that we're trying to gain by accepting Jesus as our Savior. **The purpose of having Jesus as Savior is for us to once again be, have, and do all that we could before the fall. It's stepping back into who you really are!**

Possibly you are now beginning to see how all this applies. But maybe, in spite of my explanation, you're still not fully convinced of how it can all come to pass in your own life. Hopefully, the picture will be complete as we focus on the life and sacrifice of our Lord and Savior, Jesus Christ.

JESUS CHRIST: One sacrifice, one Kingdom. Keyword: RESTORATION
Some passages to study about the believer and Jesus. Notice that I do not make a distinction here between Jesus and the believer. Why? Because the believer is One with Jesus. As you read through these verses realize that everything said about Jesus is said about you, and everything said about you is said about Jesus. These verses are all about us having our identity in Him:

We will carry the life of and live in the image of the heavenly Adam (1 Cor. 15:49), *The gates of hell shall not prevail against us* (Matt. 16:18). *We have abundant grace and the gift of righteousness, and we will reign in life* (Rom. 5:17). *If you belong to Christ, then you are Abraham's descendants, heirs according to promise* (Gal. 3:29). *Every promise in Christ is yes and amen* (2 Cor. 1:20-22). *The promise comes by faith* (Rom. 4:16). *Jesus reconciled us back to our heavenly Father, made us holy and strong in faith* (Col. 1:15). *We have been justified through faith, have peace with God through our Lord Jesus Christ* (Rom. 5:1). *We have been given the spirit from God, not from this world* (1 Cor. 2:12). *We have been given the power to forgive* (John 20:22-23). *We have been given everything we will ever need for life and godliness* (2 Pet. 1:3).

So what did Jesus come to do?

To destroy the devil's work (1 John 3:8). *To point the way to the Father by making us become sons and daughters* (John 14:6-9). *Not to condemn the world but to save it* (John 3:17). *Not to steal, kill and destroy, but to give life in abundance* (John 10:10,28). *Not to be served, but to serve* (Matt. 20:28). *To reveal the Father* (John 14:9). *To preach the good news of the Kingdom of God* (Luke 4:43).

In the next chapter we will take a more in depth look at how the finished work of Christ has restored you back to your original position in the Kingdom of Heaven. Please, read on!

Focus points and tips for success on my journey to personal thriving, the Kingdom Way:

- I know that because I am a believer, God treats me as if I never sinned and as if I am completely as I should be.
- I will never consider my obedience to God an attempt to try and gain His love. I know I am already completely loved by Him. My reason for obeying is so I can step back into who I am really created to be!

Practical reflection and consideration ('My Truth'):

Were you previously aware of the destruction that sin brought into the world? In light of what you just read, do you understand why you need a Savior?

By doing this exercise I learned about myself that:

_____

_____

_____

_____

_____

_____

_____

_____

_____

_____

_____

_____

_____

_____

_____

_____

_____

_____

_____

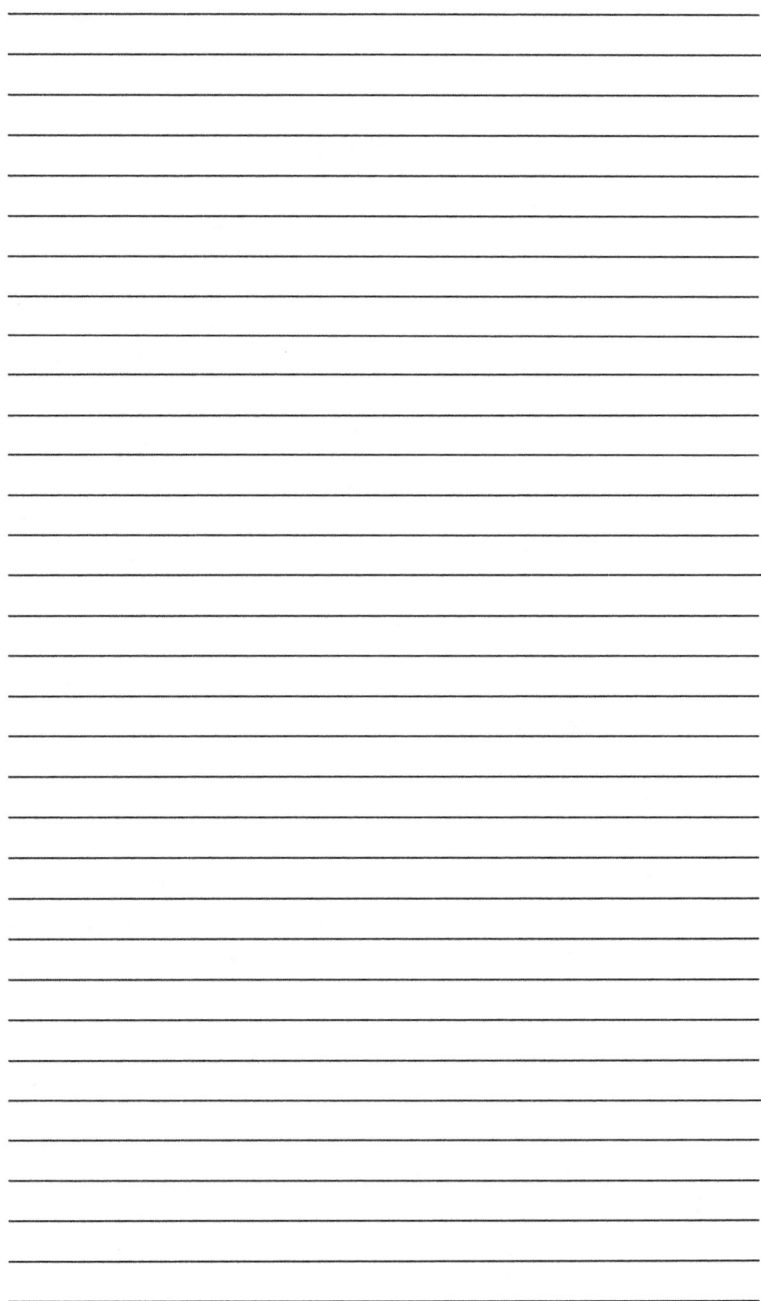

CHAPTER 4
The Life in Christ

Purpose: In this chapter you will learn how the finished work of Christ has restored you back to your original position in God. You will also learn how you can function in the Kingdom Way of life that was intended for you from the beginning of time.

We will now take a look at what Jesus did to secure our complete redemption and restoration.

Jesus came to shed His blood

In the Bible we read that sins can only be forgiven by the shedding of blood. *In fact, the law requires that nearly everything be cleansed with blood, and without the shedding of blood there is no forgiveness* (Heb. 9:22). During the sacrifices made in the Old Testament times, the blood of animals was sprinkled seven times. The rest was poured out at the foot of the altar (Lev. 4:13-21) to atone for man's sin. Jesus Christ, our perfect, ultimate sacrifice also shed His blood seven times. The rest of it flowed out of Him as He hung on the cross.

Jesus came to save the world from sin by becoming sin for us.[4] In doing so, a great exchange took place. We were forever brought back to the position of Sonship - the identity and purpose that we had before the fall; a life as if we had never sinned! Let's take a look at the seven times Jesus bled for our redemption:

1. For what we have: The first time was in the garden of Gethsemane where Jesus' sweat fell like drops of blood to the ground (Luke 22:44). Those drops of blood broke the curse that had come over the ground in the garden. By this, He allowed all those believing in Him to return to a position of tending rather than toiling for our provision. The earth was cursed in the garden of Eden, but was again restored for the believer in the garden of Gethsemane by Jesus' blood. We are redeemed to a life of **rest and abundant provision.**

2. For who we are: The second time Jesus' blood was shed was when they pulled out His beard, beat Him and spat on His face (Isa. 50:6, Matt. 27:30). Because of sin we looked nothing like the image of God anymore. But as the soldiers abused Jesus, our identity was restored. Jesus redeemed our **original beauty and identity.**

3. For our healing: Thirdly, blood was shed when they beat Jesus' back (John 19:1, Isa. 53:5). Here Jesus was wounded for our transgressions and bruised for our iniquities and we were healed by His stripes. He redeemed our **health** which we now receive by faith.

4. For soundness of mind: The fourth shedding of blood came by the crown of thorns and the beating our Savior took on His head. By allowing this, Jesus redeemed our way of thinking so that our mind could be renewed and brought back to **thoughts that are according to the Kingdom of Heaven.** Our original state before the fall.

5. For what we can do. The fifth place of bloodshed was from Jesus' hands (John 20:25). Jesus then restored and forgave every wrong deed we ever did. We were redeemed to once again do **all that He says we can.**

6. For our purpose: The sixth blood shedding was from Jesus' feet (Luke 24:36-39). Even though we may walk away from Him and enter into places and situations without Him, our walk and **purpose in life** are forever redeemed because of Christ's sacrifice for us.

7. For the healing of our hearts: And finally, the seventh time of bloodshed was when Jesus was pierced in His side and His heart (John 19:34). This last bloodshed **persuades our hearts** back again to God's everlasting truths, promises and words of life. Now our heart, which is the seat of our being and the core of who we really are, is redeemed. We can once again **see ourselves as He sees us** - being all He says we are, having all he says we have, and doing all He says we can do.

The blood of Christ was shed for **our redemption**: *In him we have redemption through his blood, the forgiveness of sins, in accordance with the riches of God's grace* (Eph. 1:7), in addition to:

Our cleansing: *How much more, then, will the blood of Christ, who through the eternal Spirit offered himself unblemished to God, cleanse our consciences from acts that lead to death, so that we may serve the living God!* (Heb. 9:14);

Our justification: *[...] and all are justified freely by his grace through the redemption that came by Christ Jesus. God presented Christ as a sacrifice of atonement, through the shedding of his blood—to be received by faith* (Rom. 3:24-25);

Our sanctification: *And so Jesus also suffered outside the city gate to make the people holy through his own blood* (Heb. 13:12);

Our life: *For the life of a creature is in the blood, and I have given it to you to make atonement for yourselves on the altar; it is the blood that makes atonement for one's life* (Lev. 17:11);

And our access to the throne: *Therefore, brothers and sisters, since we have confidence to enter the Most Holy Place by the blood of Jesus [...]* (Heb. 10:19).

Jesus came to become cursed for us at the cross

Besides shedding His blood, Jesus also became cursed for us, so that in exchange, we could be blessed. The Bible says that: *[...] cursed is anyone who is hung on a pole* (Gal. 3:13). Some translations refer to it as "a tree". When Adam ate from *the tree of the knowledge of good and evil* (the law) in the garden of Eden, he brought a curse over the entire earth. Jesus dying on a pole brought redemption and restored us back to a blessed life, free from strife.

Jesus came to restore our dead spirit

We read in Genesis that, God *formed Adam out of the dust from the ground, and breathed into his nostrils the breath of life. From that moment on man became a living being* (Gen. 2:7). God also said that the day man would eat of the 'tree of the knowledge of good and evil' *he would surely die* (Gen. 2:17). Yet we see man in bodily form still alive and well after eating from the tree.

Clearly what God meant was that man's spirit, the essence of who man was would die. So, the part which made man a living being, the spirit that originated in man died. The fallen spirit of man was no longer able to communicate with God.

For this reason, right before returning back to the Father, Jesus breathed on the disciples and said: *"Receive the Holy Spirit"* (John 20:22). As He breathed upon them they received into their nostrils the breath of life. Once again they became living beings, filled with the spirit of God, well able to commune and be in harmony with Him. This was exactly as God intended it to be when man was created.

Jesus came to show us how to live the Kingdom life by accepting God the Fathers' love

What does the Word say about God's love for us? *For God so loved the world, that He gave His only begotten Son, that whoever believes in Him shall not perish, but have eternal life (John 3:16). For the Father Himself loves you, because you have loved Me and have believed that I came forth from the Father (John 16:27). But God demonstrates his own love for us in this: While we were still sinners, Christ died for us (Rom. 5:8). He that spared not his own Son, but delivered him up for us all, how shall He not with him also freely give us all things* (Rom. 8:32)?

Jesus and The Father in Heaven are one and the same. Jesus is the perfect picture of His Father in Heaven. This means that whatever we see Jesus being, doing and having is exactly what the Father is, does and has. *Jesus answered: "Don't you know me, Philip, even after I have been among you such a long time? Anyone who has seen me has seen the Father. How can you say, 'Show us the Father* (John 14:9)? *And, the Son is the radiance of God's glory and the exact representation of his being, sustaining all things by his powerful word* (Heb. 1:3). As we develop a relationship with Jesus and look to Him we also share in His being, doing, and having (2 Cor. 3:18). This way, the Father, Jesus, and the believer become one through the 'Spirit of communion' living within us. We are connected back to our true worth, identity, and purpose.

Would you like to live the Kingdom life of thriving and not just surviving? You must then let everything you do from now on be based on an understanding of The Father's unconditional, one-way, love for you. You now have an open invitation to accept Father God's and Jesus' love, forgiveness, and cleansing which they continue to extend to you every day. You are cleansed and can break away from all the filth and limitations of the earth curse. I encourage you to enter into a relationship with Him. Get to know His love by reading the Word and looking into it for expressions of His amazing love for you.

Getting to know the Father's love will also keep you from falling into the unhealthy practice of using your faith merely to get blessings from Him. When you realize that His abundant provision and blessings are an expression of His love for you, you receive (take hold of) it and that becomes your way of responding to His great love. You no longer run after the blessings. The relationship brings the blessings with it and that's a good place to be in God! From that point on, no matter what happens in your life or what life throws at you, your relationship with Father God remains constant. You will never question His love or accuse Him when things don't go as you expect. Your life is built on your relationship and not on the pursuit of blessings.

The truth is that if we only say we belong to the Kingdom of Heaven for what we can get out of it, we will soon fall away when the road gets tough. The moment things don't go as we expect or want them to, we feel betrayed by God. It then quickly becomes evident that we were never in it for Him, but only for His gifts and blessings. Let this not be the case with us, my friends. Let's not turn the Kingdom of Heaven into some quick and easy lifestyle to satisfy our earth-cursed selfish desires.

It is so important that you understand this and stand on this firm foundation. It is on this foundation, with the building blocks of a renewed mind and an opened heart, that you can build your true identity in the Truths of God.

Jesus came to extend to us the invitation to accept Him as Lord and Savior and live the life of the Kingdom of Heaven

The Word of God teaches us that: *If you confess with your mouth, 'Jesus is Lord,' and believe in your heart that God raised Him from the dead, you will be saved. For it is with your heart that you believe and are justified, and it is with your mouth that you confess and are saved* (Rom. 10:9-10). The Word also says: *Not everyone who says to me, 'Lord, Lord,' will enter the kingdom of heaven, but only the one who does the will of my Father who is in heaven* (Matt. 7:21).

The Kingdom is all about believing and becoming a doer of the Word. After you see Jesus as He is and understand what He has done for you, you get to decide if you want to make Him the Lord (Master) of your life. You decide if you want to entrust yourself completely to Him. When you do, He becomes your Savior (the One who: saves, heals, restores, redeems, protects, provides, etc.). You then receive the Holy Spirit and cross over from the earth-cursed kingdom of this world into the Kingdom of Heaven.

Jesus came to teach us to live a life of repentance

The new life you begin from then on is a life of relationship. It is a life that is continually shaped and molded by an awareness of His amazing and unconditional love. Once we begin to grasp and internalize the reality of God's love, we understand the life of repentance. What does this mean? Jesus demonstrated and represented the Kingdom of Heaven and the character of His Heavenly Father during His walk on earth. He invited us into the life of the Kingdom with these words: *Repent, for the kingdom of heaven is at hand* (Matt. 3:2). Now all we have to do is step into that life and find out both how it works and how to work it, the Kingdom Way!

So then, the way Jesus called us to partake in His Kingdom is through **repentance, which means that we: 1. Change our** mind from the distorted belief that we have adopted about ourselves since sin entered the world, in terms of who we are, what we have, and what we can do; and 2. Conform ourselves to the Truth about what the Kingdom of Heaven says about who we are, what we have, and what we can do (Matt. 3:2, Rom. 12:2).

Remember the definition of repentance I gave at the beginning of the previous chapter? The word simply means: 'to change your mind'. Yet, for many of us, this is quite a different definition than we have thought it to be all of our life! Many seem to think that unless we grab onto the altar or pulpit in church and cry bitterly over our sins, we have not repented. But how many times have we seen this false form of repentance, even in our own lives, only to go back and commit the very thing that brought us to the altar in the first place!

No, my friend, repentance is when we change our mind about the sinful and limiting ways in which we have been walking since the fall of man. Ways of the earth-cursed system and the kingdom of this world. We need to change our mind because it has conformed to the ways of this world. We have begun considering the things of this world normal, while we call the things of the Kingdom of Heaven strange and sometimes even unattractive. Our way of thinking has become so molded to the way of this earthly kingdom that we are hardly even aware anymore that *there is a new and living way* (Heb. 10:20). It is our mind that needs to be changed, and become renewed to the things of The Kingdom of Heaven to which we belong!

I want to interject an important note here: Please realize that this life of repentance is not meant as a way to gain God's love. That was already taken care of at the cross. Because of Christ we are fully loved by the Father and nothing we do can ever change this fact! The reason we repent is to sanctify ourselves and step into the practical side of Kingdom life. As a result of our repentance, our life becomes a source of blessing and grace both to God and to those around us.

It is key for the one who calls himself a believer and child of God, and thus a child of the Kingdom of Heaven, to find out how the Kingdom operates. This is what is meant by the verse: *Seek ye first the Kingdom of God* (Matt. 6:33). We need to find out:

- What are the operating laws in the Kingdom of Heaven and how do I go about obtaining my blessings from that Kingdom (faith)?
- What do I look like according to the Kingdom of Heaven (identity)?
- What am I called to do in that Kingdom (purpose)?
- What is a normal way of life in that Kingdom (lifestyle)?

Once we get to know and become doers of the principles and laws of the Kingdom of Heaven we discover a life of thriving, and not just surviving. The Kingdom of Heaven begins to take shape within us. We will deal with this in detail in the upcoming chapters. But first, let's take a look at some distinctions between the kingdom of this world and the Kingdom of Heaven.

Examples of the kingdom of this world versus the Kingdom of Heaven

So how is the Kingdom of Heaven different to the kingdom of this world? Let's take a quick look at some distinctions:

The world says, "Hate your enemies".
The Kingdom of Heaven says, "Love your enemies".

The world says, "If you hurt me, I hurt you back".
The Kingdom of Heaven says: "Overcome evil with what is good".

The world says, "Hold onto your life at any cost".
The Kingdom of Heaven says, "Lose your life and you will find it".

The World says, "This sickness is incurable".
The Kingdom of Heaven says, "By His stripes you are healed".

The world says, "Push yourself to the top".
The Kingdom of Heaven says, "Serve if you want to lead".

The world says, "You will never make it."
The Kingdom of Heaven says, "All things are possible to those who believe".

The world says, "I am so overwhelmed".
The Kingdom of Heaven says, "My peace I give to you".

The world says, "I do not have enough. I cannot Give to you".
The Kingdom of Heaven says, "give and it will be given unto you".

The world says, "I will believe it when I see it".
The Kingdom of Heaven says, "Only believe and you will see".

Can you see the significant differences between these two kingdoms? Why did I share this with you? For two reasons:

First of all, the principles and way of life of the kingdom of this world look and feel way different than those in the Kingdom of Heaven. We need to realize this because at first it is not going to feel 'natural' to walk according to the Kingdom of Heaven.

The way to push through is to choose to obey without taking account of how it feels to your intellect or your senses. We choose to become doers of the Word. There will come a point when we realize that obedience to the Word is saying 'yes' to who we were really called to be. It then becomes easier, and even fun, to walk according to the Kingdom of Heaven. Obedience lets us step back into our true identity!

Secondly, and equally important: It is going to cost us something to live according to the Kingdom of Heaven, and the cost we will pay is our life. When we confess that we belong to the Kingdom of Heaven and that Jesus is our Lord and Savior, we make a choice to put the earth-cursed lifestyle to death. It was never meant to be ours in the first place. We die. We deny ourselves anything that is in disharmony with the Kingdom of Heaven, and say 'yes' to everything belonging to it. There is a reason why Jesus calls us to 'count the cost' when we say we want to serve Him (Luke 14:28). This implies that we recognize and agree to the terms of the Kingdom of Heaven and decide that we cannot belong to two kingdoms.

Jesus paid a high price to buy Kingdom life back for us. Let's make an honest choice either for or against the Kingdom of Heaven and stick with it, realizing that it is Life itself! So now the one question remains: Do you want to live the life of the Kingdom of Heaven?

Wait! Before you close this book because you think the cost is too high, please read on!

A new identity leading to a life of transformation
As you die to self, (meaning: the earth-cursed 'self' you were never meant to be in the first place) you live unto Him and you gain EVERYTHING the Kingdom has in it, for free! Every promise in God's Word is now yours for the taking. Jesus already paid the price for you to have it all. Isn't that awesome news? Doesn't that sound like you gain far more than you 'give up'?

Also, the instant you make Him your Lord and Savior, you become entirely who God created you to be! Your identity is completely changed and you are brought back to your original value. **The extent to which you are willing to submit to His Lordship will determine the amount of fruit that will grow in and throughout your life.** This fruit benefits both your own personal growth and that of others. From that moment on you've entered life, the Kingdom Way! The power of God and the accompanying blessings of God can now freely flow through you, causing you to see your Kingdom identity unfold day by day.

As you learn to operate under the Kingdom of Heaven, use your faith, establish your identity, walk in your purpose, and develop a Kingdom lifestyle, you begin to experience life as it was meant to be. It was meant as a life of thriving and not just surviving, no matter your past or current circumstances and experiences. During this entire lifelong process, the renewing of your mind transforms you daily into who you are according to your true Kingdom identity.

Begin today to have the Word of God, the Bible, be your Absolute Guide and resolve never to step outside of it! It's now up to you to manifest the Kingdom of Heaven in this world. Propose to remain established in your Absolute Guide. As you do, set aside philosophies of man, your own traditions and opinions and every single thing that opposes what the Kingdom of Heaven calls Truth. You have now entered the Kingdom of **Godly Truth, Godly Faith, Godly Identity, Godly Purpose and Godly Lifestyle**! Your Kingdom Life has begun!

Focus points and tips for success on my journey to personal thriving, the Kingdom Way:
- I make a conscious decision to repent (change my mind) every time I notice anything in my life that is not aligned with the Kingdom of Heaven.
- I never mix Kingdom Truth with worldly wisdom. I accept Kingdom Truth as absolute truth!

Practical reflection and consideration ('My Truth'): How do you feel when you look at what Jesus accomplished for you through His blood and at the cross? Think about ways you've lived according to the kingdom of this world during the past week. Repent! What do you notice? How easy or how difficult is it to change your mind and align it with the way of the Kingdom of Heaven?

By doing this exercise I learned about myself that:

_____

_____

_____

_____

_____

_____

_____

_____

_____

_____

_____

_____

_____

_____

PART 3
MY FAITH
Identifying and Aligning the Beliefs of My Heart

CHAPTER 5
What Is Faith?

Purpose: In this chapter you will learn to clearly identify the beliefs of your heart.

Let's begin this chapter by pointing out this Kingdom Truth: "We, believers, are created in God's image and likeness". In other words, we look like Him and do things in the same way as He does them.

So now, how did God create the world and everything in it? He did it by the spoken Word, saying: "Let there be [...]"! And it was so (Gen. 1:1-29). In the same way we are expected to bring forth into the earthly realm that which we believe in the Heavenly realm. We read in Romans 4:17 that: *God calls things that are not as though they were.* A life lesson here is that when we speak, we must always call out the solution, that which we desire to see accomplished. Not the problem!

As we proceed, here are two Bible Truths to constantly keep in mind:

Once we believed in Christ, we were given the right (freedom, legal right, authority) to become children of God (John 1:12) and now we are members of God's household (Eph. 2:19)

And here are some statements to consider and agree on concerning what we believe:

- You ALWAYS have a belief or put your faith in something. There is not a person in the world (who is in a right state of mind) who believes nothing at all. We all believe something.
- What you continually dwell on is what you choose to believe. When your mind is constantly taking you back to a particular situation or circumstance, that situation is what you have chosen to let dominate your life. It is what you believe to be true.
- Your life always reflects the beliefs of your heart. When others look at your life, what they see is what you are believing about yourself, about others, and about the world around you.
- God is not deciding today on a case by case basis if He is going to give you the inheritance of the Kingdom. Every part of your inheritance (salvation from hell, health, provision, wholeness, protection, peace, etc.) has already been given to you 2000 years ago when Jesus hung on the cross and cried: "It is finished". Believing this will propel you to live accordingly.

In light of the above statements, here's something else to think about: Let's assume that the Bible speaks the truth when it says that God cannot lie. Then, let's assume that God really says in

His Word that He has given us ALL things pertaining to life and Godliness (the entire Kingdom of Heaven with all its abundance and blessing). If this is so, would it then be safe to say that if your life does not look like the Kingdom of Heaven, the lack is on your part rather than God's? Please take the time to seriously consider your answer to this question. For, if the above statement is true, then we need to find out why we are not seeing God's promises come to pass in our life. It's time now to talk about faith.

Concerning faith. What faith is NOT:
Many believers are quick to say that they have faith, yet their so called faith is hardly able to move even the smallest mountains in their lives. So what is it that they mistakenly call 'faith', if it cannot deliver what the Kingdom says is theirs?

Let's begin by talking about what faith is NOT:
- Faith is not when we have a *strong hope* that we will get what we want.
- Faith is not when our *feelings always change* with every new experience or contrary report.
- Faith is not when we put forth a bunch of *effort* to force ourselves to create a desired result.
- Faith is not when we *try hard to believe something that we're not really believing yet*.
- Faith is not when we're living according to our own *reasoning*.

Now that we have established what is not faith, let's use God's Word to see this <u>unbelief</u> in action. As you read the two examples below, please notice the words in bold letters. What strikes you? Let's walk through and analyze these examples to understand what faith is not.

Example 1. *That day when evening came, he said to his disciples,* **"Let us go over to the other side."** *Leaving the crowd behind, they* **took him along, just as he was, in the boat.** *There were also other boats with him. A* **furious squall came up, and the waves broke over the boat,** *so that it was nearly swamped. Jesus was in the stern, sleeping on a cushion. The* **disciples woke him** *and said to him,* **"Teacher, don't you care if we drown?"** *He got up,* **rebuked the wind and said to the waves, "Quiet! Be still!"** *Then the wind died down and it was completely calm. He said to his disciples, "Why are you so afraid?* **Do you still have no faith?"** (Mark 4:35-40).

Bible quotes:	Interpretation:
"Let us go over to the other side".	Jesus' Word, His promise. The belief here should be: If Jesus says "Let us go to the other side", then it means that they will get to the other side.
They began to set out, with Jesus in the boat. A furious squall came up, and the waves broke over the boat.	They stepped out, sailed out on the Word. The contrary report.
The disciples woke him.	They let go of belief in the word resulting in turmoil and panic.

Bible quotes:	Interpretation:
"Teacher, don't you care if we drown?"	The 'prayer' of desperation where they 'prayed' the problem rather than the solution.
Jesus rebuked the wind and said to the waves, "Quiet! Be still!"	Jesus still pulls them through.
"Do you still have no faith?"	They miss out on the opportunity to see the Godly result of faith.

Example 2. *Immediately Jesus made the disciples get into the boat and go on ahead of him to the other side, while he dismissed the crowd. After he had dismissed them, he went up on a mountainside by himself to pray. Later that night, he was there alone, and the boat was already a considerable distance from land, buffeted by the waves because the wind was against it.*

Shortly before dawn Jesus went out to them, walking on the lake. When the disciples saw him walking on the lake, they were terrified. "It's a ghost," they said, and cried out in fear. But Jesus immediately said to them: "Take courage! It is I. Don't be afraid." **"Lord, if it's you,"** *Peter replied,* **"tell me to come to you on the water."** **"Come,"** *he said.* Then **Peter got down out of the boat,** *walked on the water and came toward Jesus. But when he* **saw the wind,** *he was afraid and, beginning to sink, cried out,* **"Lord, save me!"** *Immediately Jesus reached out his hand and caught him.* **"You of little faith,"** *he said,* **"why did you doubt?"** *And when they climbed into the boat, the wind died down. Then those who were in the boat worshiped him, saying, "Truly you are the Son of God."* (Matt. 14:22-33).

Bible quotes:	Interpretation:
"Lord, if it's you," Peter replied, "tell me to come to you on the water".	The prayer of faith praying the solution/the outcome, rather than the problem.
"Come".	Jesus Word, His promise. The belief here should be: If Jesus says 'come', then it means that Peter will walk and get to where He is.
Peter got down out of the boat.	He stepped out on the Word.
Peter saw the wind.	The contrary report.
Peter was afraid and began to sink.	He let go of belief in the word causing turmoil and panic.
Peter cried out, "Lord, save me!"	The 'prayer' of desperation.
Immediately Jesus reached out his hand and caught him.	Jesus still pulls him through.
Jesus said: "You of little faith, why did you doubt?"	Peter misses out on the opportunity to see the Godly result of his faith.

Without condemning ourselves, let's be honest that the above examples are some common circumstances in the life of many believers. When we do not believe or when we let go of belief in the Word or promise of God, we encounter **turmoil and panic** and our prayer, rather than being a prayer of faith, becomes a **'prayer' of desperation where we 'pray' the problem rather than the solution**. Either way, God's grace and endlessly abiding love are always there to **pull us through or help us out**. But we **miss out on the opportunity** to see the Godly result of faith in our life.

Now that we have seen this, let's take a look at what true Bible faith actually looks like:

What faith IS:
True faith is when we are **fully persuaded and fully convinced** that God's, Jesus', and Holy Spirit's Word and promise are true. We then **step out on that word** and abide in that persuasion and conviction. Also, true faith has the **ability to extinguish any contrary report**, no matter who or where it comes from.

What does the Word of God say about faith?
- *Without faith it is impossible to please God* (Heb. 11:6). We please God when we have everything the Kingdom freely promises us. It was God's great design that believers enjoy the promises of the Heavenly realm right here in the earth realm through our faith. Connected to this verse is the one that says: *It pleased the Father to give you the Kingdom* (Luke 12:32). God is pleased to give us the Kingdom with everything in it. He wants us to have it in this life and faith is the only way to get it.

- *The righteous shall live by faith* (Rom. 1:17). We have been made righteous because we believe in Christ. The characteristic of a righteous person is that we live a life of first believing, then seeing that which we have believed. We live a life of faith.
- *We walk by faith, not by sight* (2 Cor. 5:7). We don't function by the contrary reports. We hold on to faith in what God says, and God's Truth never changes.
- *Now faith is confidence in what we hope for and assurance about what we do not see. This is what the ancients were commended for. By faith we understand that the universe was formed at God's command, so that what is seen was not made out of what was visible* (Heb. 11:1-3). Those things which are unseen but real in the heavenly realm (the promises and blessings) are brought into our earthly realm by faith.
- *According to your faith be it unto you* (Matt. 9:28-29). You will have what you believe for.
- *When the son of man comes will he find faith on the earth?* (Luke 18:1-8). Jesus speaks about holding on to what you know to be yours by faith in spite of opposition. This is the kind of faith He looks for in His children.
- *"If I CAN?" All things are possible for those who believe!* (Mark 9:22-23). It's not up to Jesus anymore. He has already given us all things. It is now up to us to use our faith to take hold of what He has freely given us.

After reading the above excerpts it becomes all the more evident that we need to learn how to use our faith.

Example of <u>faith</u> in action - About getting the heart right

Mark 11:22-24 tells us: *Have faith in God, Jesus answered. "Truly*

I tell you, if anyone says to this mountain, 'Go, throw yourself into the sea,' and **DOES NOT DOUBT IN THEIR HEART** *but believes that what they say will happen, it will be done for them. Therefore I tell you,* **<u>WHATEVER</u> YOU ASK FOR IN PRAYER,** *believe that you have received it, and it will be yours.*

So prayer in God's view is: a proclamation of what you believe to be true in your heart about God's Word and His promises. Asking in prayer is saying to the mountain that which you want it to do or become. **Matthew 6:9-13** describes this to us through what we know as **'The Lord's Prayer':** *This, then, is how you should pray: "Our Father in heaven, hallowed be your name, your kingdom come, your will be done, on earth as it is in heaven. Give us today our daily bread. And forgive us our debts, as we also have forgiven our debtors. And lead us not into temptation, but deliver us from the evil one".* Notice the way the words are directed as proclamations, expressing the desired result or outcome. They are not questions, and they do not recite the problem.

The Bible goes on to say that the one who prays must not doubt in his **heart**. So, what is the heart and why is it so important in the arena of 'praying and receiving' that which we believe? We will look at this in the following chapter.

Focus points and tips for success on my journey to personal thriving, the Kingdom Way:

- I reach out to have the kind of faith that believes what God says, over and beyond anyone else or any contrary report.
- I consider it prayer when I proclaim my desired solution or outcome based on a promise from God's Word.

Practical reflection and consideration ('My Faith'):

What was your view on faith before reading this chapter? How does it compare with what you have now learned? Are there areas of your life in which you can immediately begin to activate your faith? Which Bible verses will you use?

By doing this exercise I learned about myself that:

_____

_____

_____

_____

_____

_____

_____

_____

_____

_____

_____

_____

_____

_____

_____

_____

_____

CHAPTER 6
Persuading My Heart Through Biblical Meditation

Purpose: In this chapter you will learn to align your faith with Kingdom Truth. You will learn to practice meditation so that you can begin to bring Godly results into your daily life.

The Bible mentions the heart at least 400 times. Here are some references:

- *Keep thy heart with all diligence; for out of it are the issues (boundaries) of life* (Prov. 4:23). From this verse we see that our heart decides how far 'out there' we will go in terms of what we receive from God's Kingdom. Our heart will carry us as far as its boundaries permit.
- *Out of the abundance of the heart the mouth speaketh* (Matt. 12:34). The words that come from your mouth show what you believe in your heart.
- *A good man out of the good treasure of the heart bringeth forth good things: and an evil man out of the evil treasure bringeth forth evil things* (Matt. 12:35). If your heart believes the right thing, the right thing will come out of it. Conversely, if your heart believes lies and negative reports that will be your reality.

Secular research and science now prove many truths about the heart that the Bible mentioned and knew to be true from the very beginning. It is now known that the heart is the control panel of our lives and the seat of our being. The heart is the place of our intellect, thoughts, emotions, character, love and compassion. It is the storage of our cellular memories.

Even those memories we had from the moment of conception and during pregnancy are all stored up in the heart as feelings. Later in life these feelings can manifest in diverse forms based on if they were pleasant or unpleasant. We will talk more about this in the section about 'My Identity'.

I want to show you some interesting truths about the heart according to science today:
- The heart of a fetus forms and begins to beat even before the brain begins to develop;
- The heart has a system of neurons that have short and long term memory which can affect our emotional experience;
- The heart sends more information to the brain than the brain to the heart;
- The heart sends signals to the brain that influence perception, emotional experience, and our higher mental processes;
- The heart sends out an electromagnetic field that changes according to your emotions;
- The electromagnetic field of the heart can be measured several feet away from the body;
- People around you can pick up the quality of your emotions through the electromagnetic energy that radiates from your heart.

(Source: Mind Publications and Heart Math)

Hopefully, seeing the above will help to convince you that the heart is who you really are!

Reading the following registered experiences of a few heart transplant recipients may further help you see the truth about the heart. You may be blown away by what you read. I sure was! Here they are:

- A woman received a heart transplant from a male donor who had been in a motorcycle accident. None of this information was known to her. Upon waking up she claimed she had a new and intense craving for beer, chicken nuggets, and green peppers, all food she didn't enjoy prior to the surgery.
- A man receiving a heart from a 17 year old boy suddenly picked up an intense fondness for classical music. The boy whose heart had been donated was killed in a drive-by shooting, still clutching his violin case in his hands.
- A lesbian woman was documented to have had a change in sexual orientation. Soon after getting a new heart she settled down and married a man.
- A girl who received the heart of a ten year old was plagued after surgery with vivid nightmares about an attacker and a child being murdered. After being brought to a psychiatrist her nightmares proved to be so vivid and real that the psychiatrist believed them to be genuine memories. As it turns out, the ten year old whose heart she had just received was murdered and due to the recipients violent re-occurring dreams she was able to describe the events of that horrible encounter and the murderer so well that police soon apprehended, arrested, and convicted the killer.

(Source: Theophanes: Inherited Memory in Organ Transplant Recipients)

The heart plays an important role in our life. Therefore, let us please understand how essential it is that **we learn to persuade our heart (who we really are) to embrace the right ideas**

so that the right results can flow out of our life. With this in mind, let us now turn our focus to meditation and the persuading of the heart.[5]

I first want to make you aware of some negative statements we often make. Then I want to show you how to use the Word of God to persuade your heart and counter the negative emotion associated with the first statement. Notice that both sets of statements will effectuate in your life their respective truths!

I will call this exercise: "Beliefs of the heart according to the **kingdom of this world** versus "Beliefs of the heart according to the **Kingdom of Heaven**".

We say things like: "Every morning when I wake up, I feel depressed". But, instead, we can persuade our heart to the Word of God and meditate on this promise: *Have I not commanded you? Be strong and courageous. Do not be frightened, and do not be dismayed, for the Lord your God is with you wherever you go* (Josh. 1:9).

We say things like: "I have to struggle for everything in life. Nothing comes easy".
But, instead, we can persuade our heart to the Word of God and meditate on this promise: *God's plans are to prosper me and not to harm me, to give me hope and a future* (Jer. 29:11).

We say things like: "I always get a cold when I walk in the rain". But, instead, we can persuade our heart to the Word of God and meditate on this promise: *"I will take sickness away from the midst of thee"* (Exod. 23:25).

See the difference? What do you suppose meditating on the Word of God will produce in your life? On what do YOU choose to meditate and believe? That is exactly what you will have. Guaranteed!

Now, you may say, "That sounds great but what the Bible says just isn't my reality!" Well... yes it is! You see, being in Christ makes what He says actually be your truth. We have allowed ourselves to be so swallowed up by the 'normal' of this world that we don't even realize what our reality is anymore. Just as man has done since the fall, we also use our own limited senses to decide right from wrong. Unfortunately, because of this our decisions are rarely ever based on what God says is true. The act of meditation becomes an important part in renewing our mind to what is normal in the Kingdom of Heaven to which we belong!

Yes, my friend, meditation the Kingdom Way will make your belief in God's promises become unshakeable and immovable! When we look at the definition of meditation, we see that it means: to focus one's mind for a period of time, in silence or with the aid of chanting, for religious or spiritual purposes or as a method of relaxation. The word also means 'to think deeply about something. So when we meditate we are reflecting on, pondering and rolling something over and over in our mind. Biblical meditation is when we align the beliefs of our heart and the thoughts of our mind with the Truth of God's Word.

The word used for 'mind' in the Bible has **'Imagination'** as one of its meanings. For example, the Bible says that *He [God] will keep in perfect peace whose mind (imagination) is stayed on Him* (Isa. 26:3).

The Word used for 'to know' (as in: knowing God) in the Bible is described as: to **experience with all your senses**. So, when we base our imagination on Bible scripture and activate all our senses to experience the reality of that particular verse of scripture, we are practicing what I call "Biblical meditation". The practice of Biblical meditation makes us experience life as it really is according to the Kingdom of Heaven. After we meditate we can immediately begin walking out that portion of scripture in the natural earthly realm as if it were really true, right now!

When I was ready to enter into a relationship again after my divorce, I began asking God to connect me to my new husband. I had been alone for four years by then. I based my faith on God's Word that said: *It is not good for the man to be alone. I will make a helper suitable for him* (Gen. 2:18). I concluded that there was a man out there somewhere that was alone and that needed a helper. As I prayed and asked God exactly what I wanted in my mate, I felt a strong conviction in my heart that my prayer had reached heaven and that my answer was on the way. Joy and anticipation began to fill my days. I literally began expectantly 'looking out for' the man who was to become my husband. I was that sure that I had already received by faith.

No more than two months later I received in the natural realm what God had reserved for me in the spiritual realm. I met the man God had for me. We were married within 10 months and have just celebrated our 11 year anniversary! [6]

I want to take you into a simple and practical exercise that is meant to give you a sense of what Biblical meditation looks and feels like. Let's use our imagination and our five senses and take a trip to a bakery of your choice.

Going from your current physical location to another place in this earth realm:

This exercise is best done with your eyes closed so you can really focus. But first keep your eyes open to read the instruction!

Here we go: Imagine that you walk into a bakery. As you open the door the **smell** of freshly baked bread fills your nostrils. When you walk into the store you already **see** the kind of bread you're in the mood for. You get to the counter and place your order. You **feel** the warmth of the freshly baked French bread (or any other bread or pastry you order) in your hands as you receive it from the shop assistant. You quickly break off a piece and notice the crunchy **sound** of freshness. As you put the bread in your mouth, you enjoy the delicious **taste**. You pay and walk out the door.

Well, there you go. You've just used your imagination and your five senses to experience a trip to the bakery while physically being in the exact same spot you were when you started. How did it feel to do this exercise? Did you actually smell the bread, did you see it, hear it, touch it, taste it? Did this experience actually make you want to get into your car and drive down to the bakery? That is the power of meditation, the Kingdom Way!

Biblical Meditation

Now let's translate this same example and replace the bakery with a portion of scripture from the Bible and see what happens.

Going from your current physical location to a place in the realm of the Kingdom of Heaven:

We will use Psalms 23 for this example. First take a few moments to read through it. *The LORD is my shepherd; I shall not want. He maketh me to lie down in green pastures: he leadeth me beside the still waters. He restoreth my soul: he leadeth me in the paths of righteousness for his name's sake. Yea, though I walk through the valley of the shadow of death, I will fear no evil: for thou art with me; thy rod and thy staff they comfort me. Thou preparest a table before me in the presence of mine enemies: thou anointest my head with oil; my cup runneth over. Surely goodness and mercy shall follow me all the days of my life: and I will dwell in the house of the LORD forever* (Ps. 23:1-6).

Now again, close your eyes. Picture yourself laying down in green pastures. What does that look like? How do you feel? What do you see around you? What is Jesus saying to you and what are you telling or asking Him? How does it feel when you see Him using His rod to keep ferocious animals (the devil and his demons) away from you? What is your reaction when He uses His staff to gently pull you back to the flock, after you were distracted and wandered away? What is your experience of walking through the valley of the shadow of death, knowing that He is right beside you, holding your hand?

You are now in the realm of the spirit. Experience it because this IS your reality. This IS how He is present with you always. This IS what it means to live in the spirit and walk by faith. You can now experience the truth of God's word as more real than your current earthly experience and bring that into your natural realm.

When I was still suffering through a horrible period of divorce, I remember what an instant difference it made in my life when I meditated on Isaiah 54:4: *For **your** Maker **is your husband—** the **Lord** Almighty is His name.*

I came home from church one Sunday afternoon, crying desperately because I missed my (ex)husband so much. When I opened my Bible it immediately fell on the above scripture verse.

I first was in awe that the Holy Spirit directed me straight to the very Word I needed. Once I read it and meditated on it I was spiritually moved by the reality of what God was saying. I felt myself immediately being pulled out of my pit of desperation. How awesome and what joy I experienced! The Lord God Almighty was telling me that not only was He my Maker, but my Husband as well! What better husband could I ask for? As I took some more time to meditate on this truth, peace and faith were restored right back into my life again!

This IS the life of the Kingdom of Heaven. This is where you meditate. This is how you allow your experience on earth to be as it is in Heaven!

Word-Focus Meditation

I would like to suggest another incredibly easy and beneficial way to meditate on God's Word, which I call 'Word-Focus meditation'. Let me use the first line of Psalms 23 to illustrate how this can be done. The idea is to read the entire scripture verse each time. Every time you read it, you stress a different word and allow its true meaning to sink into your heart.

Notice how I emphasize in **bold** and <u>underline</u>, the word we will focus on in each verse. Let's take a look:

<u>*The*</u> *Lord is my Shepherd,* focusing on the fact that He is **the** One and Only Lord.

The <u>***Lord***</u> *is my Shepherd,* focusing on the fact that the **Lord**, creator and owner of all things is my Shepherd.

The Lord <u>***is***</u> *my Shepherd,* focusing on the fact that He **is** now, today, this very moment my Shepherd.

The Lord is <u>***my***</u> *Shepherd,* focusing on the fact that He is **my** Shepherd, not just somebody else's, but very specific to me, tending to **my** needs.

The Lord is my <u>***Shepherd***</u>, focusing on the fact that He is my

Shepherd, the Shepherd who walks with me, the Shepherd who tenderly guides and leads me, the Shepherd who protects me from evil.

Do you get the idea? Can you fully experience the Word of God opening up to you and carrying you into the Kingdom realm that is yours today? Use this Word-Focus way of meditating for every Bible verse and quickly find yourself aligned with your true identity in Christ and all that He holds in store for you!

I invite you to practice this way of meditation and begin to shape your life into what God has designed it to be. You will experience the reality of the Kingdom way of thriving, right here and now!

I close off this chapter with a prayer that is similar to that of Elisha in 2 Kings 6:15-17. 'That the eyes of every believer may be opened to truths we cannot yet see with our natural eyes'. We need to know that the Truth of the Kingdom of Heaven is very real in the spiritual or Kingdom realm. It is waiting to be tapped into and brought into the realm of our daily earthly experience. Let's make a commitment to believe that God's Word is true and real.

Once our heart is persuaded by meditation, we no longer doubt. We speak the truth which we believe, granting us whatever we ask for in prayer! True Biblical meditation will certainly help push us another step further toward thriving and not just surviving in our personal life, the Kingdom Way! Is this not a life worth dying for?!

Focus points and tips for success on my journey to personal thriving, the Kingdom Way:

- I am aware that I am who I am in my heart.
- I am careful about the words I speak from my heart because I realize that my heart will do everything it can to make sure those words become my reality.

Practical reflection and consideration ('My Faith'): Think about one negative confession you usually make about your health, your circumstance, your work, etc. Identify your true heart beliefs that lie at the root of these negative words. How does it feel to recognize and be aware of what you are really believing in your heart? What portion of God's Word can you meditate on to counter that negative belief?

By doing this exercise I learned about myself that:

_____

_____

_____

_____

_____

_____

_____

_____

_____

_____

_____

_____

_____

_____

_____

_____

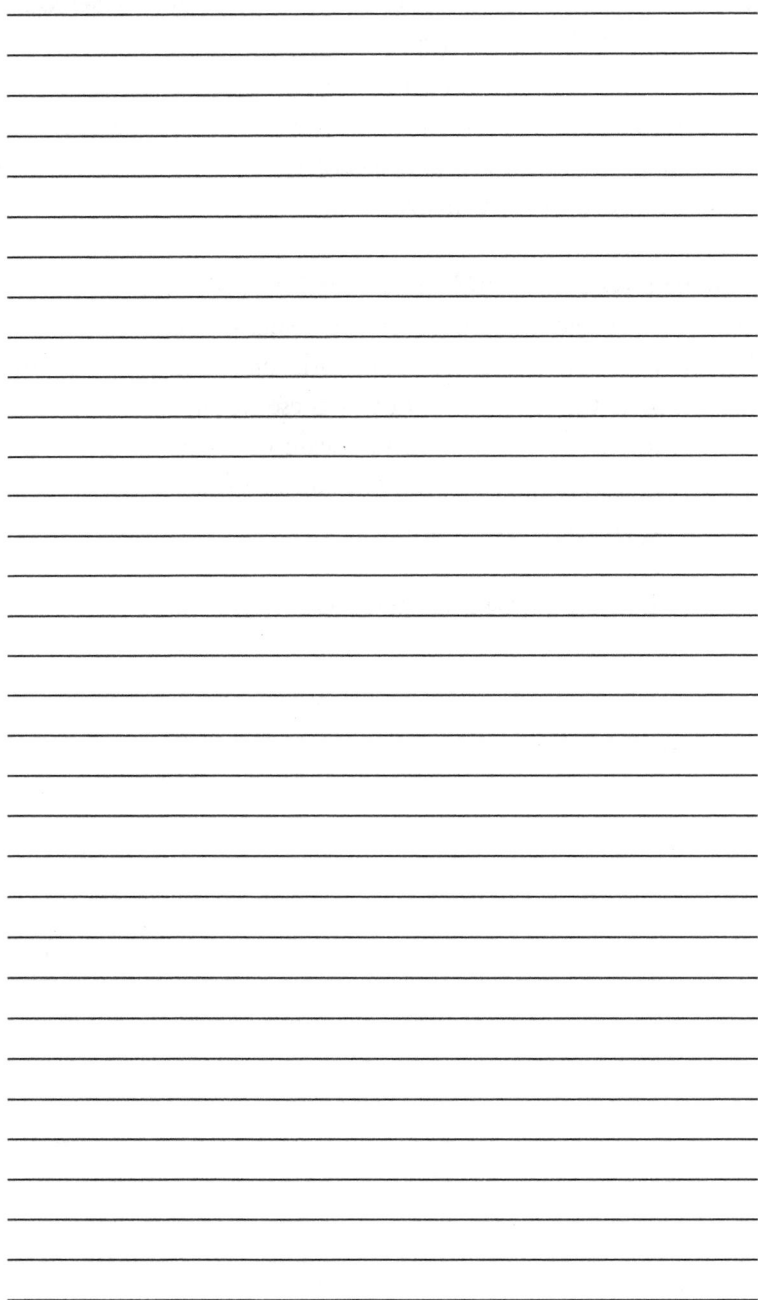

PART 4
MY IDENTITY
Shaped By Man or Decided By God?

CHAPTER 7
My Identity According to the Kingdom of Heaven

Purpose: In this chapter you will learn to see your true identity.

Identity [7] is described as the fact of **being** or the **characteristics** determining who or what a person is. Based on this definition let's begin this chapter by identifying who we are and what are our characteristics according to the Kingdom of Heaven.

According to the Bible we have been created in the **image** and **likeness** of God. We are also **blessed**, and **destined to reign**. *And God said, Let us make man in our image, after our likeness: and let them have dominion over the fish of the sea, and over the fowl of the air, and over the cattle, and over all the earth, and over every creeping thing that creepeth upon the earth. So God created man in his own image, in the image of God created he him; male and female created he them. And God blessed them, and God said unto them, Be fruitful, and multiply, and replenish the earth, and subdue it: and have dominion over the fish of the sea, and over the* *fowl of the air, and over every living thing that moveth upon the earth* (Gen. 1:26-28).

Let's pull these terms apart and see what we come up with.

1. **When the Bible talks about our image, it means** we look like God, so I am who He says I am.
2. **When the Bible talks about our likeness, it means** we act like God, so I can do what He says I can do.
3. **When the Bible talks about our being blessed and destined to reign and have dominion, it means** we have everything that's needed to reign in life. So, I have what He says I have.

So, who am I, what can I do, and what do I have according to the Kingdom of heaven? Let's take a close look at some scripture verses and what they say about our identity.

Who I am: All through the Bible, reference is made that I am a son or daughter of the most high God, My home is in Heaven, My Father is a King to whom all things in the entire Universe belong. I AM called by His name!

I am a child of God (John 1:12). *I am light of the world* (Matt. 5:14). *I am a friend of Christ* (John 15:15). *I am chosen by Christ* (John 15:16). *I am a new creation* (2 Cor. 5:17). *I am a fellow citizen with God, a member of God's household* (Eph. 2:19). *I am righteous and holy* (Eph. 4:24). *I am loosed from the power of satan* (Col. 1:13). *I am fully accepted in the beloved* (Eph. 1:6). *I am more than a conqueror* (Rom. 8:37). *I am fearfully and wonderfully made* (Ps. 139:14). *I am in this world, as He is in heaven* (1 John 4:17).

What I have: Think about it. Heaven, with everything good in it, belongs to me. I don't need to ask for permission to take anything. It has all been paid for and given to me by Jesus! Just as a mature child in an earthly family, I have right of entry and access to the Kingdom of Heaven as I so desire. It belongs to me! I really do have all that the Kingdom of Heaven says is mine!

I have a place in the heavenly realm (Eph. 2:6). *I have forgiveness of sins and I receive God's abundant grace* (Eph. 1:6-8). *I have Christ living in me* (Eph. 1:27). *I have His divine power granting me all things, pertaining to life and godliness* (2 Pet. 1:3). *I have God's great and precious promises so I might participate in His divine nature* (2 Pet. 1:4). *I have eternal life in Him* (John 3:15). *I have life in abundance* (John 10:10). *I have been engraved in the palm of His hands* (Isa. 49:16). *I have His guidance* (Ps. 73:24). *I have all my needs supplied according to His riches in glory* (Phil. 4:19). *I have His peace that passes all understanding guarding my heart and mind in Christ Jesus* (Phil. 4:7). *I have been blessed with every spiritual blessing in the heavenly realms in Christ Jesus* (Eph. 1:3).

What I can do: I can do everything in which I have faith (belief). The key to entering and having access to my heavenly home and its blessings is my faith. I can be unshakably convinced and fully persuaded that I really am able to do all that the Kingdom of Heaven says. So whatever I desire to do, I first seek to find out if God says I can. If He does, then I know I can!

I can call those things that are not, as though they were (Rom. 4:17). *I can call it out by faith and see it be on earth as it is in heaven* (Matt. 6:10). *I can no longer live for myself, but for God, because I am already dead* (2 Cor. 5:14-15). *I can put off the old man, renew the spirit of my mind and put on the new man* (Eph. 4:22-24). *I can do all things through Christ who gives me strength* (Phil. 4:13). *I can have everything when I believe* (Mark 9:23).

Realize that the above list of scripture regarding our true identity is in no way complete. There is much more said in God's Word about who we are, what we have and what we can do because of our faith in Jesus Christ. Please take the time to read through that awesome love-letter of God called The Bible to know what He says about you and practice being just that - of course through meditation!

Focus points and tips for success on my journey to personal thriving, the Kingdom Way:

- In my true identity I look like God, I act like God and I have what God has. I live consciously aware of this truth by saying 'amen' ('it is so') and stepping into the reality of it.
- I choose to believe and live every word spoken by God about who I am, what I have and what I can do, as if it is true right now. Because it is true in the realm of the Kingdom of Heaven, I know it is true for me now.

Practical reflection and consideration ('My Identity'): Take some time to reflect on what you have always thought about yourself in terms of who you are, what you have, and what you can do. How does it compare with what God says about you in these areas? How can meditation help you accept God's truth above the self-image you have created?

By doing this exercise I learned about myself that:

_____

_____

_____

_____

_____

_____

_____

_____

_____

_____

_____

_____

CHAPTER 8
Consequences of a Skewed Identity

Purpose: In this chapter you will learn how to establish yourself in your Godly identity so that you can be freed from every negative experience that has produced destructive and limiting beliefs in your life.

In spite of what God says about us and who we are in Him, we don't always see the truth of God's Word reign supreme in our lives. Why is that? Because sin and the kingdom of this world have caused our view of ourselves to become skewed. We lose sight of who we really are and of who God called and made us to be.

Sin and the effects of the fallen world (the kingdom of this world) produce wounds and lies in us that mis-shape our identity and affect our heart beliefs. Remember that the heart is the control panel of our lives and the storage place for all our cellular memory. The heart even remembers those events that took place during the early moment of conception. Therefore, the negative experiences which have affected us during the course of life need to be deliberately dealt with at a heart level. If not, they will continue to haunt us and make for a crippled and dysfunctional life in which we will always struggle to thrive.

Before getting into the two ways to heal our heart and subsequently our life, lets look at how misconceptions can occur in our heart beliefs, which then produce negative life experiences. I apologize beforehand to those of you who may encounter some painful memories or triggering as we go through this list. I promise you that I will provide practical aid later on in this chapter. For now, let me say this: I understand that life may have been tough for you - very tough! But no matter what you've been through, no matter what blows life has dealt you over the years or who has harmed you, realize this: In Christ we all have the same opportunity to begin our walk anew on equal ground.

Thanks to the finished work of Christ on the cross and the shedding of His blood, we all stand on equal ground. The person with the 'great life' no longer has the advantage over the one who grew up in hurt. You have an equal opportunity to believe in Christ's finished work and profess Him as your Lord and Savior. As you do, you become a new creation in Him and every harm done to you in the past is washed away. The offenses as well as their impact on you are all forever removed. You no longer need to be that person, for that is not who you were created to be in the first place. God sent His Son to heal and restore His children back to their original position, created in His image and likeness, blessed and destined to reign.

Reach out to the new life He offers you today. Bury your past in Him and begin to thrive, the Kingdom Way! Let me show you how. Take my hand, let's take the plunge!

Our identity can become skewed:
1. At conception or during pregnancy: because of the circumstances surrounding your mom's life at the time. You may have been conceived by way of incest, rape, or another form of sexual abuse. Maybe your mom was sexually or physically

abused when you were conceived or during her pregnancy. You may have been the 3rd, 4th, 5th, ... child. Your parents may have been worrying about how in the world they could provide for yet another child. Maybe while being sexually active your mom was thinking: "I hope I don't get pregnant". Yet she did become pregnant with you.

Any or all of the above circumstances can produce misconceptions and beliefs of the heart like: "I am always afraid"; "nobody wants me (around)"; "I feel rejected"; "I am unworthy"; "I hate myself"; "I hate people"; "I never have enough"; "I always do the wrong thing"; "I want to please others at all cost"; "I am angry"; "I can never say what I really feel and think".

2. At the time of birth: Your mom may have passed away at delivery or shortly after. Maybe you were born breached, with the umbilical cord around your neck, jaundiced, or premature. Maybe you came into the world by use of forceps or a vacuum pump. Or you may have been abandoned or put up for adoption right after birth.

Some misconstrued feelings and beliefs of the heart in this case could be: "I do everything backwards"; "I can't get ahead in life"; "Things keep getting worse"; "I feel lonely"; "I am isolated"; "What now?"; "I can't face life alone"; "I feel stifled"; "I feel choked"; "If I move forward I will experience (emotional or physical) pain"; "I always have to fight for everything in life"; "Nothing comes to me easy"; "I am too little to make it out in a big world"; "I am rejected"; "I don't know who I am"; "I am unworthy"; "I am always wondering: 'what's going on?'"; "I always expect something bad to happen to me".

3. When growing up in the family:
Father: You may have grown up in a home with an emotionally

or physically absent or abusive father. Maybe your father did not adequately provide for the family; was jobless; did not encourage, support and protect you; or spoke destructive words to you.

Mother: Maybe your mother was very controlling; or had to work two or more jobs to make ends meet; and/or for whatever reason was not there to comfort you and take care of your daily needs. Maybe because she was resigned to a sickbed your mom was not there to answer your questions as a young child growing up.

Brother and sisters: You may be part of a blended family and/or you may possibly know about the existence of other siblings but not have much contact with them. Maybe you couldn't get along with your siblings and there was constant fighting and arguing among you. You could have grown up in a family where there was noticeable favoritism and unjust division of privileges between siblings. Maybe you were seldom included in the activities of your siblings.

These experiences may have led to feelings that could ultimately make you have a distorted view of yourself, of others and of the world around you, like: "I resent myself and others"; "I am afraid to try new things"; "I have no sense of identity"; "I over-please"; "I live in survival mode" (take anything I can get); "I have to provide for myself because no one else will"; "I don't fit in anywhere"; "I feel isolated"; "I don't deserve good things so why try?"; "I can never do anything right"; "I can't figure out life or get a handle on life"; "I know no one wants to spend time with me"; "I will never be accepted"; "I will remain passive"; "I'm always the least"; "I never get the attention I want or need"; "I feel unjustly accused".

4. Out in the world: negative words, negative experiences, bullying at school or work, divorce, being held back for having ambitions, joblessness, childlessness, loneliness, other life calamities... These experiences can negatively affect your feelings and outlook on life, and you may begin believing things like: "I live a life of regret"; "I am guilty"; "I am worthless"; "I have low self-esteem"; "I am lost"; "My life is over"; "I want to commit suicide"; "I know good things never last".

All the above negative thoughts and feelings of the heart can easily lead to **actions of self-sabotage** or a destructive and limiting lifestyle if left unchecked.

Actions of self-sabotage

I think this is a good place to emphasize once again that we are who we believe to be in our heart. Whether or not it is to our benefit, that which our heart tells us is the truth from which we will live our life. Period! The above examples show that our heart can be affected even from the early moment of conception and from then on throughout our lifetime. If the **skewed and distorted views and beliefs of the heart** are not consciously dealt with they will continue to plague us and stunt our growth, even when good things and **opportunities** present themselves.

It is not for nothing that the Word of God admonishes us to *'Keep your heart with all diligence, for out of it* (the heart) *flow the issues* (boundaries) *of life* (Prov. 4:23). In other words, you get as far in life as your heart will allow you to go. Willpower may carry you a great way. Still, if your heart beliefs are skewed, you will be brought right back to the place of your heart boundary when willpower fails you.

You can also become frustrated as you attempt to go over and beyond your heart boundary. Why? Because your heart has not yet expanded to the capacity of true belief to sustain you in that new place. I hope this explanation enables you to see the importance of dealing with the true beliefs of your heart.

Now that we have established the importance of the heart, let's take a look at a practical example of self-sabotage. Let's say you meet a great guy or girl and you have the chance to develop a deep, meaningful and long lasting relationship (**opportunity**). While things are going fine between the two of you, your heart may be thinking one or more of the following thoughts (**skewed and distorted beliefs of the heart**): "Having a good relationship is not possible for me"; "I don't deserve this person"; "My relationships always start off great, but then suddenly come to an end"; "No one in my family has ever had a relationship for more than two years, so what makes me think I will?" etc.

Over time, you may notice that suddenly strife, contention, and constant arguing become the norm in a relationship that was once so satisfying. Or you reach the 'two year mark' and you suddenly begin to hate the person you were once so crazy about (**actions of self-sabotage**).

What is the reason for this and how does this all happen? The answer to this question is found in Mark 11:23. This is a verse we already dealt with in an earlier chapter, where Jesus teaches: *"Truly I say to you, whoever says to this mountain, 'Be taken up and cast into the sea,' and does not **doubt** in his heart, but believes that what he says is going to happen, it will be granted him"* (good or bad).

Your heart is the seat of your being. Your heart is the place of your true beliefs. Your heart has the capacity and function to always protect and bring to pass that which you believe deep inside.

The word **doubt** means that we believe something else more than we believe God's Word. When we believe a lie, a negative experience, or limiting words spoken by ourselves or others more than we believe what God says in His Word, we get what we believe. The heart will see to it that we do!

In order to thrive and not just survive in life, it is of utmost importance that we find out what it is we really believe in our heart. If our belief does not align with God's Word about **who we are, what we have and what we can do**, we immediately repent (change our mind). Then we train our heart (through knowing the truth and by way of meditation) to believe and live the truth of the Kingdom of Heaven. This is how we begin to expand our heart capacity to believe, receive and maintain God's perfect will for our life.

The Word of God is the source of all that God has promised. As we read the Bible we learn more about what is normal for a child of the Kingdom and we begin to integrate it into every area of our life.

In the next chapter I want to address how we can help support our heart in believing God's Word. We will see how the art of forgiveness and the acceptance of our God-given authority help us continuously reflect the life we've been called to lead.

Focus points and tips for success on my journey to personal thriving, the Kingdom Way:

- I recognize the power of self-sabotaging beliefs and I choose to re-program them by believing God's Word more than I believe my circumstances and experiences.
- I expand the boundaries of my heart by meditating daily on God's Truth.

Practical reflection and consideration ('My Identity'): Do you recognize anywhere your identity may have been skewed? Can you see areas in your life where this has led to actions of self-sabotage? What scripture verse can you use to counter this?

By doing this exercise I learned about myself that:

_____

_____

_____

_____

_____

_____

_____

_____

_____

_____

_____

_____

_____

_____

_____

_____

_____

_____

CHAPTER 9
Restoring My Skewed Identity

Purpose: In this chapter you will learn how to apply forgiveness so that you can live free from wounds and lies.

In order to establish God's image and likeness in our life at a heart level, we will need to forgive those people who have offended or sinned against us. Let's begin by looking at two important words.

Forgive: to send away

Sin   : to miss the mark, an offense

Jesus teaches that *if we forgive the sins of any, their sins have been forgiven them; if we retain the sins of any, they have been retained* (John 20:23). In other words, it is up to us to decide whether we choose to send away or retain both the offense done against us and the negative feeling associated with it. Retaining sin, or holding on to sin, will make our life unfulfilled and unhappy. When we carry the burden of both our own sins and the ones done against us, we are unable to live freely. We also block the flow of blessings from the Kingdom of Heaven. When we choose to send away sin (forgive) we are able to replace wounds and lies with God's truth. We begin to see His blessings flow in and throughout our life.

For those of you who have a hard time forgiving, I want to help make you aware of two things: First of all, the reason you forgive is for you, not for the offender. When you choose to remain in a state of unforgiveness, you are in prison. You are the one feeling bad every time you think of or see your offender. You are the one suffering when you replay that offense in your mind over and over again. You are the one angry and unable to sleep at night. You are the one making yourself physically and emotionally sick. All this time your offender is probably not even aware of the havoc his or her offense is causing in your life. Forgiveness is the key that enables you to unlock your prison door from the inside and set yourself free!

Forgiveness is a powerful tool that God has given us to live a life of freedom. Besides that, choosing to forgive detaches you from the situation and allows God to intervene and have His will carried out in you, the offender and the situation!

Secondly, I believe that forgiveness becomes 'easier' when we realize that 'wounded people wound people'. You see, when people are not aware of God's precious love for them, they fail to understand their own true value. Therefore they are equally incapable of understanding the value of others. So, resolve to not allow sin in others to produce sin in you. In other words, do not offend because others have offended against you. Live according to your God-given identity, where forgiveness is a normal way of life.

Once you make the decision to forgive you can actually lift up your hands to heaven, as if handing something to the Lord, and pray: "Father God, I hand you now this file of evidence containing every **offense** done to me by this person. I hand you every **negative feeling** that these offenses have caused in me. As I hand these to you Father God, I ask you to deal with *(name)* as you see fit. I now take a step back and release him/her into Your hands. From this day forward I choose not to deal with these offenses anymore. I choose to live in the truth of who I am in You".

Let's say you are dealing with depression as a consequence of abuse. Here is what I want you to do: Every time the devil brings the memory of the offense back into your mind (and believe me, he will), you say: "I have given that situation of abuse (the offense) to the Lord and I choose right now to be joyful." What you are doing here is focusing on a positive feeling that is the opposite of how the offense made you feel. You make yourself consciously aware that you are choosing to accept who you really are as your positive truth. You can even help yourself by asking Jesus this question based on 1 John 4:17: "Jesus are you depressed, hopeless, angry, offended right now sitting at the right hand of the Father?" The answer will always be: "No!", and then you can say: "Then neither am I, because your Word says that as You are in Heaven, so am I in this world. I choose joy, hope, peace." Do you understand?

I will give you some more practical examples of forgiveness later on in this chapter, but for now I hope this serves you. Let us continue to look at some other interesting truths!

Implementing the art of forgiveness
The reasons we choose to forgive are twofold: 1. We forgive in order to walk free from wounds and lies (past and present), and 2. We forgive in order to restore and/or maintain a healthy relationship with the Godhead (Father God, Son, and Holy Spirit).

Forgiving in order to walk free from wounds and lies
The first reason we forgive is to be able to walk free from wounds and lies (past and present). In order to achieve this, we meditate on Bible verses related to the areas of our life where we want to see specific results. Casually read the Bible and be aware of those portions you have difficulty accepting as truth. This is a good exercise to discover those places where you may need

to extend forgiveness. When you have difficulty embracing a portion of God's Word, it is often because someone in your life has at some point offended you. As a result, you have retained the offense and allowed it to have more power than the truth of God's Word. It has caused a distortion in your feelings and your belief system. [8]

As you read the Word with the purpose of freeing yourself from wounds and lies, never go digging for answers. Just see what Holy Spirit shows you as you casually commune with Him through His Word. Once He does, deal with the situation according to what I am teaching you here.

Allow me to give you an example of what I call my 'Personal Shades'. With this I will illustrate how to use the Word of God to identify wounds and lies and deal with what Holy Spirit reveals to you. I first want to ask you a question: "Have you ever noticed how ten people could read the same scripture verse and everybody gets something different out of it?" Why is that? It is because we each read the Bible wearing our own 'Personal Shades'.

When we read scripture we all bring our own personal life experience into it. In doing so, the Word speaks to us and touches us right at the point of our need. God, by His Holy Spirit, can then begin to work on our behalf in our heart by way of restoration. He brings healing, admonition, encouragement, or whatever else we may need. He is a personal God and communicates with us through His Word. As we respond, we engage in a meaningful two-way relationship with Him.

Be aware that the Word of God does not consist of dead letters on a page. No, *it is living and active* (Heb. 4:12) and very intimate. It is our Father seeking to commune with us, His beloved children, and bring us into alignment with who we are according to His Kingdom. Isn't that awesome? So, decide to use the Word as a way to have a conversation and receive restoration from your Heavenly Father!

We will now look at how God's Word can serve as a tool for forgiving those who have caused distortions in our belief system. An example: Growing up people have been telling you: "You will never amount to anything in life". Then you read the passage of scripture where God says: *For I know the plans I have for you, declares the LORD, plans to prosper you and not to harm you, plans to give you hope (a pleasurable expectation of good) and a future* (Jer. 29:11).

As you read this scripture you notice that your heart is unable to embrace this truth. You have always heard and accepted the lie that 'you will never amount to anything in life...'. When you encounter that, stop and pray: "Father, Jesus, or Holy Spirit (which ever one you prefer): "Show me who I need to forgive". And when He shows you who has harmed or offended you, pray: "I choose to forgive *(name)* for bringing into my life the lie that I will never amount to anything. I send away the offense and the ungodly feelings that this lie has caused in my life."

Once you identify these feelings, begin to send them away (forgive) one by one. For example: "Feeling of inadequacy, low self-esteem, strife (or whatever is the case in your situation), I send you away now! You do not belong in my life and I do not accept you!" Then take time to actually feel these negative emotions flow out from you. Keep calling out every negative emotion you encounter during the process and send them all away.

Once you experience peace, say: "Lord, I thank you for Your Word being my reality. I thank you now for creating me to prosper and to have the hope of a good future. Notice this is all said in present tense because this is who you are NOW. You may want to write down what God shows or speaks to you.

Meditate on the truth of the Word as you have learned previously until it really becomes the new reality from which you live. The idea here is to re-program your heart back to the truth of the Kingdom of Heaven. You repent by changing your mind about what you have accepted as normal (the lie) and choose to believe that the truth is as God says it is.

Depending on the situation, you may also need to forgive yourself. Be sure and take the time to do so, without condemning yourself. I encourage you to read God's Word in this way from now on. Live by it and re-align yourself with your God-given identity in Christ.

Forgiving in order to restore and/or maintain a healthy relationship with the Godhead

I mentioned before that there is a second reason why we forgive. It is to restore and/or maintain a healthy relationship with the Godhead (Father God, Son, and Holy Spirit). Let me explain. In the book of Genesis we see the concept of 'family' introduced for the very first time. The family, consisting of father, mother, and children, is the institution established by God to be an earthly representation of the communion between Father God, Jesus, and Holy Spirit. Problems often arise when negative experiences within the earthly family causes a distorted view of the Godhead.

In the previous chapter we looked at some things that could possibly negatively affect a child while growing up in the family. I now want to briefly explain how negative experiences within the earthly family can cause misrepresentation of the Godhead. I will then explain how to heal the wounds and lies that can result. I want to explain this by way of a concept that I refer to as the **'Family-Trinity'** - a model consisting of three parts:

1. Throughout the world it is still commonly accepted as truth that in the earthly realm the father is the one mainly responsible for shielding us from harm (**protector**), working outside the home to meet our needs (**provider**), and impacting our life by his words of encouragement and edification (**identity**). Throughout the Bible we see Father God referred to as having these qualities.

2. It is still commonly accepted as truth that in the earthly realm the mother in the family is mainly responsible for being there to answer most of our questions while growing up (**teacher**), consoling and hugging us when we get hurt (**comforter**), and taking care of our daily needs (**nurturer**). We read in the Bible that these roles are also attributed to Holy Spirit. (**Note:** I am NOT saying that Holy Spirit is a woman. Please do not misunderstand! What I am saying is that some of the key characteristics of a mother are also found in the description and function of Holy Spirit in the Bible).

3. It is commonly accepted as truth that our siblings (and friends, if there are no siblings) are the ones we talk to about practically everything (**communication**). They are the ones with whom we butt heads and go out and have fun (**companionship**). In God's Word, we see Jesus fulfilling these roles as He interacts with His disciples and followers.

As you look at this model, ask yourself: Could it be that it was God's plan for dad to be an earthly representation of God the Father? For mom to be an earthly representation of Holy Spirit? For our siblings to be a representation of Jesus Christ in this earthly realm? Could it be that when God looks upon the family on the earth He is hoping to see a reflection of the relationship and communion between Himself, Jesus, and Holy Spirit, coexisting in love and harmony? Indeed, I believe that it was meant to be that way!

Unfortunately, it does not always happen that way. Children grow up not understanding how God the Father could ever want to be their provider because dad never did! They don't understand how God could ever call them His beloved because dad sure never showed that he cared. When children grow up they can't imagine why in the world Holy Spirit would ever want to take time to teach them anything. Why would He? Mom worked two jobs and was never around to answer questions. Or they don't understand why Jesus would ever want to spend time with them, since in their case siblings always left them home by themselves.

Do you understand? Can you see how the picture of the Godhead can get skewed because of misrepresentation within the earthly family? When wounds and lies occur, our hurt and hardened hearts keep us away from God. We just never got a clear picture of who He is and how much He really cares and wants to be a part of our life.

Let me clarify here that I am not at all implying that your dads, moms and siblings were bad people. Because, maybe your dad was extremely proud of you but he himself never learned how to verbally express his feelings, so he never told you how he felt.

Or maybe your mom had no choice but to work long hours to provide for you since dad wasn't there. Maybe your brothers did want to play with you, but mom sent them outside because she couldn't handle the noise of all the kids being together in the house at the same time.

Notice that your perception of the situation may not even have been accurate. Still, even so, the negative feelings associated with what you perceived were real, and may have caused a distortion in your view of God! So you see, it's not about pointing fingers and faultfinding. It's about getting wounds and lies out of the way so you can connect with the Godhead in a healthy way.

We need to get our relationship with Father God, Jesus, and Holy Spirit healed so that we will always be confident that we can turn to Him anytime and for anything. Once we do, He shows us that He still thinks we're amazing, even after making that stupid mistake. He shows us that He still wants to be our comforter when we feel hurt and alone. He lets us know that He still wants to be our best friend, even after we turned our back on Him and purposed to go our own way.

How much we miss out on the love of God when we don't understand that He really is and wants to be to us all that He says in His Word! Let's rid ourselves of an unhealthy perception of the Godhead. Let me teach you how!

Forgiveness is a tool we must use to restore our relationship with the Godhead. I personally know someone who had to learn to forgive her dad for sometimes making her promises, but not always coming through for her. As her relationship with Father God became more intimate, she began noticing that she never really expected to get what she asked Him for. She never believed that He would actually come through for her. Sometimes she didn't even bother to ask Him anything. This was a misperceived view of Father God as a result of the relationship with her earthly dad.

This lie was so subtle that it went unnoticed for years. But then one day she became aware. Once she did, she took herself through a process of: 1. granting forgiveness to her 'offender' (in this case; her dad), 2. Renouncing the lie that God would make her a promise and not keep it, and finally 3. Allowing Father God to begin speaking Truth into her life. She has since developed an incredibly strong belief that God will always do what He promised. She based this on His word that He is God and cannot lie. The scripture verse is found in Numbers 23:19 where God says: *God is not a man, that He should lie, Nor a son of man, that He should repent; Has He said, and will He not do it? Or has He spoken, and will He not make it good?*

You can use the 'Personal Shades' illustration and follow the steps for setting yourself free. Let's suppose the person telling you 'You will never amount to anything in life' is your dad. You read the passage of scripture where God says: *For I know the plans I have for you, declares the LORD, plans to prosper you and not to harm you, plans to give you hope and a future* (Jer. 29:11), and notice that your heart rejects this truth. The only thing you hear constantly ringing in your ears are your dad's destructive words.

As soon as you encounter this situation, stop and pray: "I choose to forgive my dad for telling me that I will never amount to anything in life. I forgive him for making me feel small and insignificant. I forgive him for making me feel that I have to work twice as hard to prove myself", etc. (You know your feelings. Pour them out to God in an expression of forgiveness toward your 'offender').

Then pray: "Father God" - or "Holy Spirit", or "Jesus, Son of God" depending on what wounds and lies you're dealing with, [9] "I renounce the lie that You think I'm unable to make it in life. I renounce the lie that I always have to fight to achieve anything good." Then finally you ask: "Father God, what is the truth You want me to know?" Now sit silently in His presence and let His Words wash over you and tell you exactly how He sees you and what He thinks about you.

Sometimes you may experience that your mind wants to fight and deny the words that God is speaking to you. When this happens, thank Him in a loud voice for the truth He has imparted to you. Keep repeating it to yourself until the lie is flushed out by God's awesome truth. At other times you may hear a voice of condemnation. If you are a child of God, you can immediately reject this voice. It is never God, for the Bible says: *Therefore there is now no condemnation for those who are in Christ Jesus* (Rom. 8:1). Repeat this truth to yourself. You may want to write down what God tells you and use this as a basis for your personal time of meditation.

Clear? I really hope so, because this will absolutely change your outlook on life and on who God is to you! You are now ready to learn more about how to establish the blessings and destiny of God in your life. This will be our focus in the next chapter.

Focus points and tips for success on my journey to personal thriving, the Kingdom Way:

- As I commune with Holy Spirit by reading the Bible, I allow Him to show me the wounds and lies I have accepted as part of my skewed identity. I deal with them through forgiveness.
- I no longer allow misperceptions in my family relationships to cloud my understanding of the love of God the Father, Jesus and Holy Spirit.

Practical reflection and consideration ('My Identity'): Do you have a hard time forgiving those who have offended you? How will what you learned in this chapter make forgiveness easier for you? How is your connection with God the Father, Jesus and Holy Spirit? Can you trace this back to distortions in your relationship with your father, mother or siblings?

By doing this exercise I learned about myself that:

_____

_____

_____

_____

_____

_____

_____

_____

_____

_____

_____

_____

_____

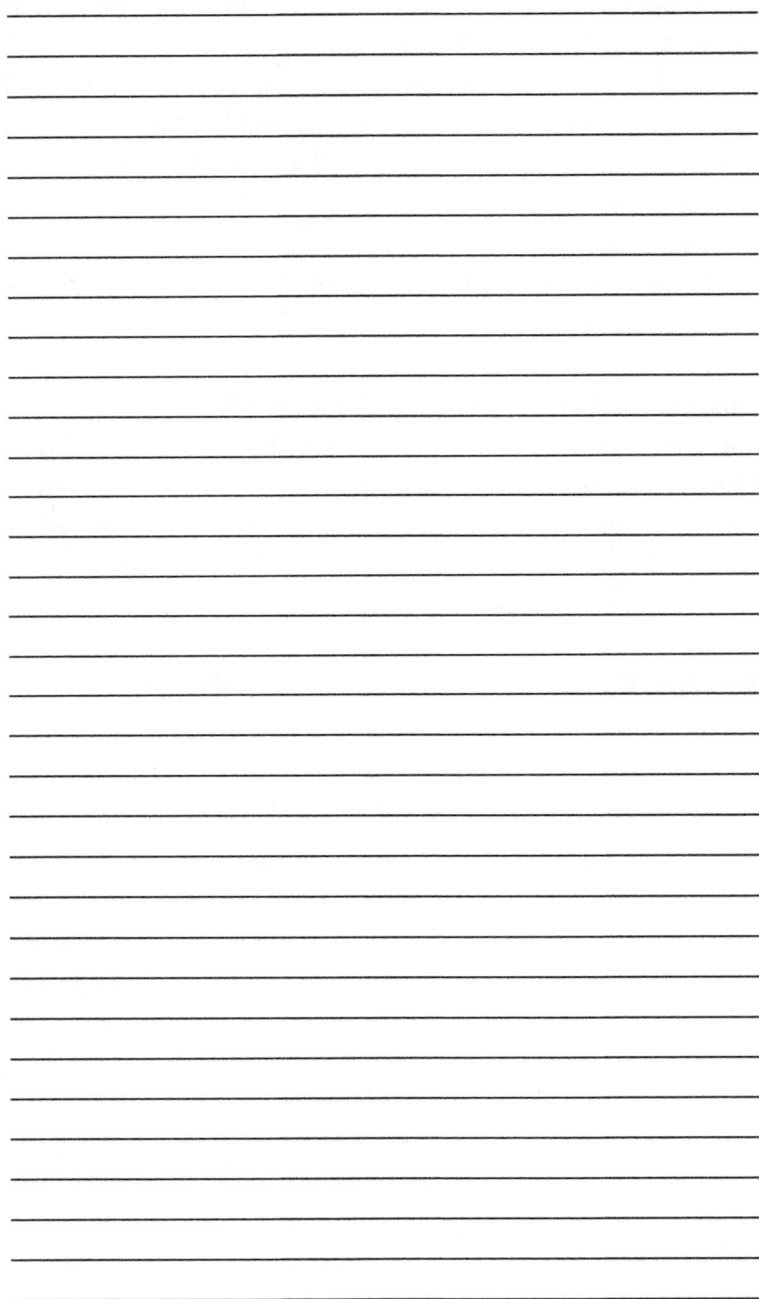

CHAPTER 10
Exercising My God-given Authority

Purpose: In this chapter you will learn how to embrace in your heart the blessings and destiny God has chosen for you. You will learn to use your God-given authority to take hold of what legally belongs to you.

In this short chapter we will briefly discuss authority and legality in God's Kingdom.

Authority [10] is your legal right, liberty, or power.
I want you to read a story with me, found in the gospel of Luke. It is about Jesus healing a woman, a daughter of Abraham, who was bent over for 18 years. Jesus said to the people that as a daughter of Abraham she had **a right to the promise of healing**. We see that the reason she had that right was because of who she was: **a daughter!**

On a Sabbath Jesus was teaching in one of the synagogues, and a woman was there who had been crippled by a spirit for eighteen years. She was bent over and could not straighten up at all. When Jesus saw her, he called her forward and said to her, "Woman, you are set free from your infirmity." Then he put his hands on her, and immediately she straightened up and praised God. Indignant because Jesus had healed on the Sabbath, the synagogue leader said to the people, "There are six days for work. So come and be healed on those days, not on the Sabbath." The Lord answered him,

"You hypocrites! Doesn't each of you on the Sabbath untie your ox or donkey from the stall and lead it out to give it water? Then should not this woman, a daughter of Abraham, whom Satan has kept bound for eighteen long years, be set free on the Sabbath day from what bound her?" When he said this, all his opponents were humiliated, but the people were delighted with all the wonderful things he was doing (Luke 13:10-17).

Now with this in mind, you must understand that your current position is that of **son or daughter of Abraham, son or daughter of Father God**. Because of this, you too have the legal right to every promise - yes, EVERYTHING - that Jesus died and resurrected to obtain for you. You have the right to the entire Kingdom of Heaven, which includes every blessing and every promise spoken by God. So why should you not receive (take hold of) all that is yours right now?

Does the Bible not teach us that we are now members of the household of God (Eph. 2:19)? What does being a member of an earthly household look like? What does it look like to be a child - I'm not talking about a baby here, but a child who is at a responsible age - growing up in a home? Do you have to sheepishly ask if you can sleep in your own bed? No, you jump right into it any time you want! Do you have to ask if you may please partake of the meal that is served up at dinner? No, you pull up your chair, sit down and eat! Do you need permission to take a drink from the refrigerator? No, you open the refrigerator, pop the bottle cap and drink! What belongs to the household belongs to you!

This is the same for us, the children of the Kingdom of Heaven. Everything that is available in the Kingdom is yours. Because you are in Christ you belong to the Kingdom of Heaven, and the Kingdom of Heaven belongs to you. Please, understand the magnitude of this truth and enter into what has been freely made available to you through Christ! This is who you are. It is your identity. You are a member of the household of God!

Hopefully by now you are saying, "I want this!" To which I say, "If you are in Christ you already have this!" If this is what you desire, allow me to show you that these blessings are already part of your reality.

Take a look around as you stand in that Heavenly household of which you are now a member. What do you see? Is there darkness? Is there fear? Is there need? Is there sadness pain or jealousy? What do you see?? It's all positive. It's all light and life, isn't it? And it's all yours, my friend! What you now need to learn is how to enforce your legal right and take hold of what belongs to you!

First of all, always be aware that things like sickness, scarcity, depression, fear, anger, etc. are NOT legal in the life of a Kingdom Child. Reject them. They do not belong to you! They belong to the earth-cursed system that Jesus died and resurrected to free you from Do not ever accept them as part of who you are.

What we do accept and embrace are truths and qualities like: life, health, joy provision, peace, restoration, abundance, protection, blessing, and so on. This IS YOUR LEGAL RIGHT! The Bible says that you have been given the keys (authority) of the Kingdom of Heaven. We use these keys to bind everything in our life that is not according to the Kingdom of Heaven and release everything the Kingdom says we are, have, and can do! (Matt. 16:19). As you use your authority to bind and release, be fully aware that all of heaven is behind you.

Secondly, use your faith. Be fully convinced that the promises are intended for you and then agree with the Kingdom of Heaven (believe) that they are yours in Christ (2 Cor. 1:20).

Then begin to *call those things that are not, as though they were* (Rom. 4:17). This means that before you see the manifestation of God's promise in your life you begin to speak them as if they are true right now. This is the confessing of the Word. You are saying what God says about you and your situation.

A friend of mine who is a true faith warrior tells the story of her daughter who called to ask if she could borrow $150 from her mom. She had a pressing need. The daughter was in dire straits with no financial prospects. My friend was unable to wire money to her daughter at that time, but what she could do was pray. So pray she did! She used her authority to call out and release finances for her daughter. She began rebuking need and scarcity, because it did not align with the Kingdom of Heaven in her daughter's life. Shortly after pronouncing the "Amen", my friend received a call from her very surprised daughter. She had just received $150 up front from a lady who suddenly appeared at her doorstep and placed an order for one of the products the daughter made. The amount she received was exactly what she had asked her mom to borrow!

So from now on, let's decide to be fully aware of our legal rights in Christ. We consider anything that does not align with the promise of the Kingdom of Heaven to be illegal and deal with it accordingly! God has provided us with the tools to do so.

Focus points and tips for success on my journey to personal thriving, the Kingdom Way:

- I see myself as part of the household of the Kingdom of Heaven. I realize that I have free access to everything that's available in my Kingdom home.
- I immediately reject every feeling or experience that is not in line with the Kingdom of Heaven. I consider it illegal, bind it's power, and release what God says I am, have, and can do.

Practical reflection and consideration ('My Identity'): The Bible calls The Kingdom of Heaven your home. Not when you die, but right now! How does it feel to realize that you are actually part of God's household? How does it feel to know that, as a child of God, you can boldly access everything in it? What would you like to have from your heavenly home?

By doing this exercise I learned about myself that:

_____

_____

_____

_____

_____

_____

_____

_____

_____

_____

_____

_____

_____

_____

PART 5
MY PURPOSE
Entering into My Destiny Freed from the Bondage of Toiling

Chapter 11
About My Provision and My Purpose

Purpose: In this chapter you will learn the laws of The Kingdom of Heaven for prosperity and abundant provision.

Purpose[11] is described as the reason for which something is done or created or the reason for which something exists. Have you ever asked yourself why you exist and what is your purpose for being alive at this particular time? Some people never ask themselves this question and are not at all concerned about it. In their opinion, they just live life... and at a certain time they die.

Others do think about it. Yet sometimes they fall into the trap of allowing the enemy to use past wounds and lies to keep them from God's best. God's purpose for their life is never fulfilled. Once the devil gains entry in this way, he will do everything in his power to try and keep us believing lies. In the end the lies become self-fulfilling prophecies causing need and mediocrity. We do not have to let this happen, however. We can allow the light and truth of the Kingdom of Heaven to shine upon us. God has freed us to walk in the fullness of our purpose and destiny despite our past experiences!

The last kind of people are the ones who KNOW they have been created for something great. They know they have a mission to accomplish and a destiny to fulfill, but their financial burdens prevent them from doing so. Too much time is spent trying to find adequate provision for themselves and their families and they are unable to fulfill their life's purpose.

There is not much I can offer those who have no interest in living their destiny, so, I will not spend time trying to convince them. However, for those who are interested in realizing their greatness, I will use this chapter to teach you how to be free from worldly financial bondage so that you can embrace your God-given purpose.

About our provision and our purpose

I would like to submit to you that there is a clear connection between finding provision and finding your purpose. Let me explain what I mean. I think it is essential for children of the Kingdom of Heaven to realize that provision and prosperity are both included in our salvation. When Jesus said "Your faith has saved you", He meant: "Your believing in me with all your heart (faith) has brought you salvation meaning: healing, blessing, deliverance, provision, prosperity, etc.".

If we don't understand this truth, we will run after and pursue provision and prosperity according to the ways of this world. We will struggle and operate under the laws of this earthly kingdom. When we do this it proves that we have not yet realized that provision has already been given to us as part of our salvation in Christ. This struggle for survival, my friend, is what the Word of God refers to as "toiling". Toiling is seeking for provision within the earth-cursed system and according to the system of this world. In doing so, we will never get ahead, and subsequently never accomplish that for which we have been created. Let's set out to learn how to avoid the trap of toiling.

As with anything else, understanding some foundational truths will quickly put what I'm talking about here into perspective. Only then can we clearly see God's plan. I want to take you back for a moment to the very first beginnings of toiling. Please read the first three chapters of Genesis, so you can answer the following questions along with me.

Let's look at the first few chapters of the Bible and see how life was supposed to be. Then let's see what happened when every good thing was lost through sin. As you read Genesis chapters 1, 2, and 3, focus especially on the following verses: Genesis 1:6, 9, 14, 20, 24, 26, 27, 29; - Genesis 2:1, 2, 7, 8, 15, 21, 23; - Genesis 3:8, 10, 16, 17, 18, 19, 23. I believe you will experience a massive shift in your heart and mind once you get to the last question in the following sequence. Let's answer them and discover what we were made for!

1. What was man's first job description before the fall (Gen. 2:15)? Answer: His job description was to tend the garden. To <u>tend</u> is to care for or look after, to give one's attention to, to wait on as an attendant or servant.

2. What became man's job description after the fall (Gen. 3:17-19)? Answer: *His job description became to toil. Cursed is the ground because of you [...] by the sweat of your brow and painful <u>toil</u> you will eat from it all the days of your life.* **To toil** is to work extremely hard or incessantly, to move slowly and with difficulty by exhausting physical labor.

3. Did God consider toiling a blessing or a curse? Answer: Toiling is a curse. The Word of God says: Because you listened to your wife and ate fruit from the tree about which I commanded you, 'You must not eat from it, *'Cursed is the ground because of you; through painful toil you will eat food from it all the days of your life* (Gen. 3:17).

That was a dark day for all mankind. For when Adam fell, we were all brought under the curse of sin. But thankfully God had a plan! He offered us a way back to the Godly position we had before the fall! When Jesus died at the cross, everything, including our abundant provision in God was restored back to its original state for us who believe! What exactly happened at the cross? Let's clarify this by answering a few more questions.

4. Did Jesus become cursed for us? Answer: Yes, He did. For it is written that *Christ redeemed us from the curse of the Law, having become a curse for us - for it is written, "CURSED IS EVERYONE WHO HANGS ON A TREE in order that in Christ Jesus the blessing of Abraham might come to the Gentiles, so that we would receive the promise of the Spirit through faith* (Gal. 3:13-14). Also, the Bible teaches us that Jesus' sweat fell like drops of blood to the ground. When this happened, the cursed ground was restored for every believer. Christ exchanged that which was cursed into blessing for us. *And being in agony He was praying very fervently; and His sweat became like drops of blood, falling down upon the ground* (Luke 22:44).

5. What is the promise that we received? Answer: we were promised a life in God's Sabbath rest. This means that rather than toiling we are promised abundance and overflow, causing us to have more than enough. We no longer have to sweat and toil and run after provision. *For the one who has entered His rest has himself also rested from his works, as God did from His. Therefore let us be diligent to enter that rest, so that no one will fall, through following the same example of disobedience* (Heb. 4:9-11).

6. What did God do after He finished creating the world and everything in it? Answer: He rested. God created a perfect world for us. After that, He created us as perfect beings in His image and likeness. After His labor, He rested. *Thus the heavens and the earth were completed in all their vast array. By the seventh day God had **finished the work** He had been doing; so on the seventh day **He rested** from all his work. Then God blessed the seventh day and made it holy, because on it He rested from all the work of creating that He had done* (Gen. 2:1-3).

7. What did Christ say after He bore all our sins and curses at the cross? Answer: He said, 'It is finished'. Jesus had done everything necessary to restore us back to our original position and created value. He restored our Godly image and likeness. Later, *knowing that **everything had now been finished**, and so that Scripture would be fulfilled, Jesus said, "I am thirsty." A jar of wine vinegar was there, so they soaked a sponge in it, put the sponge on a stalk of the hyssop plant, and lifted it to Jesus' lips. When He had received the drink, Jesus said, **"It is finished."** With that, he bowed his head and gave up his spirit* (John 19:28-30).

8. What is Jesus now doing at the right hand of the Father? Answer: He is seated (resting) after finishing His work. *Day after day every priest stands and performs his religious duties; again and again he offers the same sacrifices, which can never take away sins. But when this priest (Jesus) had offered for all time one sacrifice for sins, **he sat down** at the right hand of God* (Heb. 10:11-13).

9. What are the children of the Kingdom called to do?
Answer: We are called to rest in the finished work of Christ.
Adam and Eve were created on the 6th day after everything was
put in place for them to enjoy. God had finished all the work
for their provision and pleasure before He made them (Gen.
1:26). We, as children of the Kingdom of Heaven are called to
live in the already finished work of Christ. We can rest in all
that Christ accomplished for us at the cross and through the
shedding of His blood. We are called to enjoy His fullness and
provision and everything He obtained for us. *For we who have
believed enter that rest* (Heb. 4:3).

**10. If you know and understand the above truths, then my
last question is: Why are you still toiling?** Answer: ..... (fill in
the blank).

I realize that many of you were never taught how to break free
from a life of toiling. As a result, you have accepted it as a normal
part of life. I invite you to please keep reading. I want to show
you an escape route that you may have never heard mentioned
in this way before.

Let's quickly look at the Kingdom Way to get out from under
the curse of toiling. I hope by now it's becoming clear that
God NEVER intended for you to toil to find provision. Your
purpose from the very beginning was to receive God's Kingdom
provision by faith. You are called to a life of purpose and
glorifying the name of your Father in Heaven. You were created
not for toiling, but to be about the Father's business.

The first truth you must decide to believe is that 'it is finished'!
Therefore if you belong to the Kingdom of Heaven, toiling is no

longer part of your 'job description'. *For we who have believed enter that rest* (Heb. 4:3, 10-11).

The second truth is that you must commit to believing that it is **illegal** for you, a child of the Kingdom of Heaven, to toil.

Thirdly, repent (change your mind) about toiling. Experience by meditation what your life of abundant provision looks like in light of the Kingdom of Heaven to which you belong. Based on the Word of God see yourself in your current situation **tending instead of toiling**. What does that feel like, look like, etc.? As learned in previous chapters, meditate in God's Word, engaging your five senses to make this Kingdom Truth real to you.

Finally, get to know and understand the operating **principles and laws** of the Kingdom of Heaven as a means to your guaranteed provision. Allow me to show you how in the next chapter dealing with God's secret weapons for continued provision.

Focus points and tips for success on my journey to personal thriving, the Kingdom Way:

- I know that I am created for tending and will not accept toiling as my job description one day longer!
- I use meditation to open my heart to the limitless possibilities of having continuous provision by tending rather than toiling.

Practical reflection and consideration ('My Purpose'): Have you accepted toiling as a normal way of life? Do you now see that was never God's intention for you? How will that change the way you view your work? What can you do differently?

By doing this exercise I learned about myself that:

_____

_____

_____

_____

_____

_____

_____

_____

_____

_____

_____

_____

_____

_____

_____

_____

_____

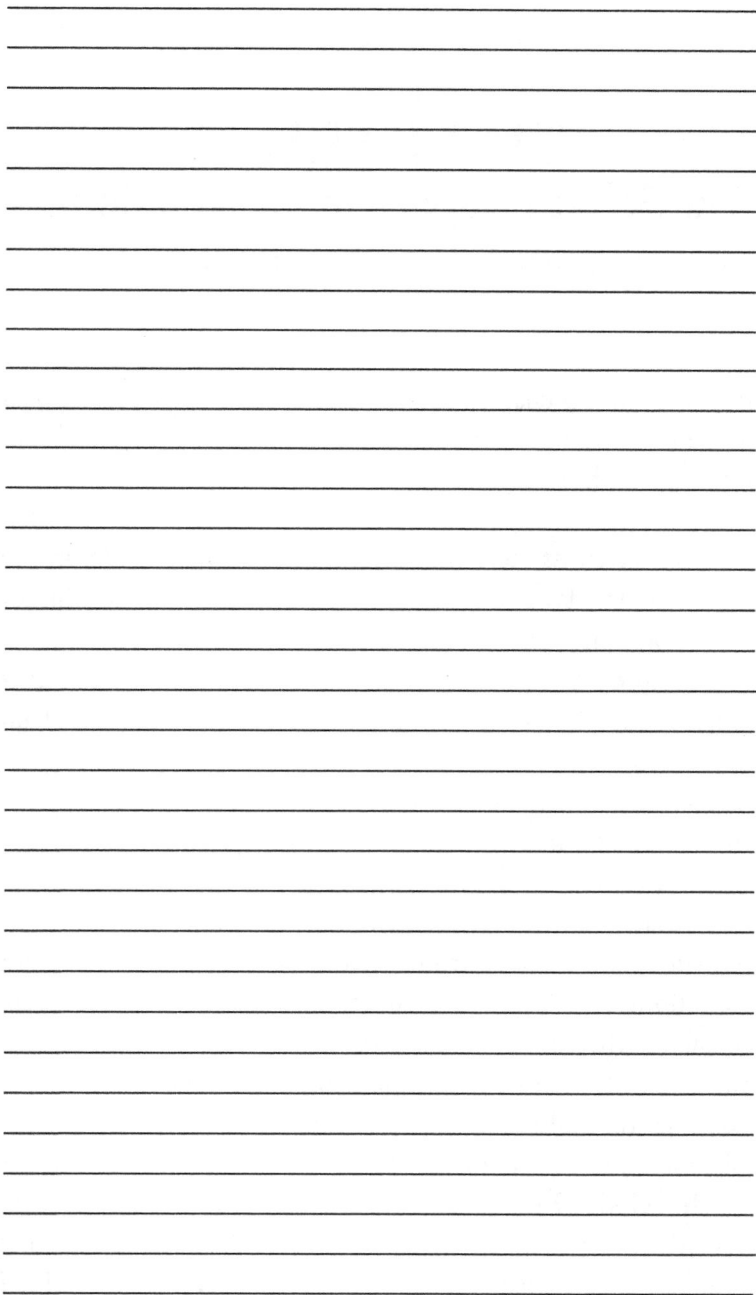

CHAPTER 12
The Secret Weapons of the Kingdom of Heaven for My Continued Provision

Purpose: In this chapter you will learn about God's master plan for getting you out of the earth-cursed realm of toiling and into His ongoing heavenly provision.

God has given us secret weapons for our provision. Before we look at them, I want to help you understand the meaning of two important words: *principles and laws.*

A principle [12] is a <u>fundamental truth</u> or proposition that serves as <u>the foundation for a system</u> of belief, behavior, or for a chain of reasoning.

A law [13] is a statement of fact, deduced from observation, to the effect that a particular natural or scientific phenomenon <u>always occurs if certain conditions are present</u>.

These two definitions show that principles and laws are fundamental and basic truths that always occur once the right conditions are present. This means that laws and principles are constant. They always remain the same. Because of this, laws and principles can be re-produced time and time again. In our example, the right 'condition' that needs to be present for the 'phenomenon' to occur is our faith!

In God's Kingdom there are always certain laws in operation. For example, the laws of: believing and seeing, giving and receiving, sowing and reaping. Please, keep this in mind as I continue building my case against the sin of toiling. Let's look at some background information to get a better understanding of our position and rights in Christ!

The 'problem' - The fallen world: no longer as God created it to be

I will now take you step by step through a quick overview:

1. Adam and Eve were originally given dominion and authority over the earth. **Dominion** is to rule over, to be lord over, to dominate, and to reign. Until the fall of man, Adam and Eve enjoyed their God-given rulership. They tasted what future generations were supposed to have (Gen. 1:26, 28).

2. Adam and Eve disobeyed God and ate from the tree of the knowledge of good and evil. In doing this, Adam transferred all his God-given dominion and authority over to God's enemy, the devil. This truth is confirmed in the passage of scripture where Jesus is tempted by the devil in the wilderness. *The devil led Jesus up to a high place and showed Him in an instant all the kingdoms of the world. And he said to him, "I will give you all their authority and splendor; it has been given to me, and I can give it to anyone I want to. If you worship me, it will all be yours"* (Luke 4:6).

Notice that Jesus did not question the devil or say that he was lying. Jesus knew that it was true that all authority had been handed over to the devil by Adam. Though we are children of the Kingdom of Heaven, the earth still suffers under the curse of sin. Yet, because of the redemptive work of Christ, ALL dominion and authority has been put back into the hands of Jesus. *And Jesus came up and spoke to them, saying, "All authority has been given to Me in heaven and on earth"* (Matt. 28:18). Jesus in turn made this authority available to every believer in Christ!

God also created a way for children of the Kingdom to escape the effects of the earth curse of toiling and running after provision. This is where the principles and laws of the Kingdom of Heaven become really important for us. Let's watch!

What was God's way of solving the provision-dominion issue for His children? Answer: He gave us two secret weapons - tithes and offerings. We often don't like to talk about this topic of tithes and offerings, but... continue on this journey with me! I believe you'll soon be jumping for joy at your Heavenly Father's insight and masterful plan. With this He perfected a way to get us out from under the earth-cursed system of the devil and back under God's blessing. In this chapter I will only briefly touch on the topic of tithes. I will use most of my time teaching you God's wisdom for using your offerings as a way of escape from toiling.

Secret Weapon 1: Our offerings

Jesus taught us about a secret weapon that the devil cannot touch! He teaches us not to build our security around having possessions of this earth. We are also not to gather provision in the same way the world does. It is not God's plan to have us operate under the curse of stress and hoarding to get our needs met. That way of obtaining provision belongs to the devil and is the way of the kingdom of this world. Besides causing us strife while still leaving us unsatisfied, at best it is a false and temporary sense of security.

I want to read with you what Jesus intended for the children of God's Kingdom and then look at some practical application.

In Luke 12:22-33 we read the words of Jesus: *"For this reason I say to you, do not worry about your life, as to what you will eat; nor for your body, as to what you will put on. For life is more than food, and the body more than clothing. Consider the ravens, for* *they neither sow nor reap; they have no storeroom nor barn, and yet God feeds them; how much more valuable you are than the birds! And which of you by worrying can add a single hour to his life's span? If then you cannot do even a very little thing, why do you worry about other matters? Consider the lilies, how they grow: they* **neither toil nor spin***; but I tell you, not even Solomon in all his glory clothed himself like one of these. But if God so clothes the grass in the field, which is alive today and tomorrow is thrown into the furnace, how much more will He clothe you? You men of little faith! And do not seek what you will eat and what you will drink, and do not keep worrying. For* **all these things the nations of the world eagerly seek***; but your Father knows that you need these things. But* **seek His kingdom, and these things will be added to you. Do not be afraid***, little flock, for your Father has chosen gladly to give you the kingdom.* **Sell your possessions and give to charity***; make yourselves money belts which do not wear out, an* **unfailing treasure in heaven, where no thief comes near nor moth destroys.***"

As you read this, what do you think it means? Do you think God does not want us to have 'things'? No, not at all! What it does mean is that God wants His children to obtain provision by finding out how the Kingdom of Heaven operates. He does not want us going after it according to the ways of the world. He wants us to detach from worldly ways rather than clutch onto them. He teaches us to give away rather than hold on to. This is how we secure provision the Kingdom Way! We see this expressed in the Words of Jesus: **"Sell your possessions and give to charity"**. That is when we will have an endless flow from the Kingdom of Heaven into our lives (**'unfailing treasure in heaven'**). Now that we see this, let's look at how to practically apply this truth into daily life.

I want to look at five Bible stories where we are taught to place the little bit that we DO have into the hands of the Kingdom of Heaven or a representative thereof. Please read the following scripture verses with me and let's talk about the similarities in each.

The stories we will be looking at are: The five loaves and the two fishes (Matt. 14:13-21, John 6:1-13), A small jar of olive oil (2 Kings 4:1-7), A handful of flour and some oil (1 Kings 17:10-14). We will also look at the story of Peter and his fishing boat from Luke 5:1-9 in a slightly different yet comparable context.

Let's take a look at some highlights from these stories. The question asked in each one of these accounts is: What do you have? God is asking you: What can you give Me (God) to work with? What is the seed you are able to sow? Do you only have five loaves and two fish to feed a multitude of 5000 men? Bring it to Me. Do you only have one jar of olive oil left in your kitchen cupboard? Bring it to Me. Do you have flour and oil, just barely enough to bake your last cake for your family? Bake that last cake and bring it to Me!

You see, God invites us to bring and to sow whatever we have, no matter how small. Sow it into the Kingdom of Heaven just as the disciples brought the bread and the fish to Jesus; just as the widows brought their flour and oil under the dominion of the prophets Elijah and Elisha (representatives of the Kingdom of Heaven). Whatever you bring to God is transferred and passes over from the dominion of the earth-cursed system of this world into the dominion of the Kingdom of Heaven. Changing dominions makes what little you have come under the dominion of the Kingdom of Heaven. In that Heavenly realm abundance is normal way of life. This is the Kingdom in which we were created to live, untouchable from the enemy! Come on! Do you get it? What do you think about that?!

Let's go back to the story of Peter and his fishing boat, a symbol of his business and a vehicle for securing provision. We read in Luke 5 that Jesus borrowed the boat after Peter had been out fishing all night and caught nothing. After Jesus was done teaching from the boat, He instructed Peter to go into deep water and throw out his net. The catch of fish was so large that even Peter's companions profited. He had to call for their help and the boats almost sank under the weight of the provision.

Now, does that not sound like abundant Kingdom provision? I believe there is a strong suggestion in this story. Here is my interpretation: When we offer our business as a platform to spread the message of the Kingdom, we receive specific instructions and strategies from Heaven for the growth and blessing of our business.

Notice that in the examples above, bread was multiplied into bread, oil into oil, fish into fish. Nowhere does it talk about money. What is money multiplied into when it is brought under the dominion of the Kingdom of Heaven? Money could multiply into money, but it could also 'become' whatsoever else you need it to be!

Let me explain: The difference between money and the bread, the oil, and the fish is that money is a means for bartering. You can sow money and bring it under the dominion of the Kingdom of Heaven. You then receive back from the Kingdom an abundant provision to get your needs met in any area. This could be your groceries, your rent, a car, paying a doctor's bill, debt cancellation, and so on. Why? Because money can represent ANYTHING you need!

As you may have noticed, what we are talking about here is a law. Namely, the law of sowing and reaping. Remember that if it is a law, it will always work under the right conditions (faith).

In light of this, here are some easy steps to follow to access your Kingdom provision from the Heavenly realm, as God intended:

a. Decide what it is you need from God.

b. Take your seed, bless it (set it apart from the earthly kingdom and bring it under the realm of the Kingdom of Heaven).

c. Sow the seed into the Kingdom of Heaven (this could be a ministry or foundation that is serving the cause of the Kingdom. It can also be individuals or groups of people who have need, etc.). As you sow your seed, name it. For example: "For my rent".

d. When you pray, declare that you believe that you receive. Pray: "Father, I believe that I receive____ and I release my faith now for 'my rent'.

e. If you are believing for provision together with your partner, pray the prayer of agreement according to Matthew 18:19 which says: *"Again I say to you, that if two of you agree on earth about anything that they may ask, it shall be done for them by My Father who is in heaven."*

f. Write down what you are expecting to receive and date it. Leave an open space to write when and how you received your provision. I encourage you to take God at His Word and begin to see the truth of the Kingdom of Heaven manifest in your life today!

My husband and I once sowed into a certain ministry, asking God for a good second-hand Toyota Forerunner. We asked that the price be 30% cheaper than a brand new one. We were trusting God for a bargain. We held our seed in our hand, blessed it and sowed it while proclaiming that it was 'for our car'. We prayed the prayer of agreement together and declared God's promises over our seed. We thanked God that the car was already waiting to come our way.

No less than 9 days after, we received our shining red Toyota Forerunner with relatively few kilometers on the teller. And the price? 30% less than that of a brand new one!!! God is fully able and wants to provide our every need. Let's decide to take Him at His Word and trust Him to do for us just what He says.

Life experience shows that provision comes to us in mainly one of three ways:
First of all the provision can come by multiplication of the seed. In this case it immediately fills the existing need, as in the example of the loaves and the fishes.

Secondly, the seed can first be multiplied, after which the Lord gives specific direction on how to invest it for a greater and long term increase. This is seen in the example of the widow who filled the jars of oil and was then instructed by Elisha to sell the oil to pay her debts.

Thirdly, God can show you where the opportunities are and give instructions on how to reel it in. Compare this to Peter who was instructed by Jesus to 'go out into deep water and throw his nets out'. The catch was so immensely large that others were even able to share in the profit!

Three things to remember:
1. When you pray, always bear in mind that faith is the key.
Therefore, make sure you are relying on faith when you pray. Test your heart to know if you're really believing what you're asking God for. If not, go ahead and wrap your faith around something 'smaller'. Something which you ARE actually able to embrace as truth by faith. Don't be ashamed. Don't strain and force. Allow yourself time and experience to grow in your faith.

As you see blessing in the smaller things, your faith will slowly (or rapidly!) be stretched until you dare to believe God for the impossible. Everything begins with a first step. Can you imagine yourself with your needs met? Is the faith there? Once it is, begin to thank God and believe that you receive.

2. Continue acquainting yourself with the faithful and loving character of God every day. As you get to know Him better, it becomes easier to believe that He will actually give you what you have asked Him for. Why? Because you become familiar with His love and character. You learn that His abundant provision is a gift to you and that He sent His Son to die so that you could have it all.

3. Remember that Kingdom children never run after provision. We receive or gather it by faith! My friends, what will our life look like once we grasp and begin to apply these principles of the Kingdom of Heaven? I feel a sense of limitlessness. How about you? What are these truths releasing inside of you?

Let's proceed quickly to touch on the subject of the other secret weapon: our tithes

Secret Weapon 2: Our tithes

The giving of tithes is another way God provided for His children to break out of the earth-cursed system and into the abundant supernatural provision He intended. I will not spend too much time on this. The two key scripture verses on the topic largely speak for themselves. Genesis 14:18-23 and Malachi 3:10-12.

In Genesis 14:18-23 I want to focus your attention on two words: **'A tenth' (tithe),** which is translated in the Aramaic language as **'maaser'** and, **'rich',** which is translated in Aramaic as **'aser'**. Notice that the word 'aser' is hidden in the word 'maaser'. This implies that our having riches is hidden in the giving of our tithes. Enough said, right? What an incredibly awesome God we have! This really is totally amazing to me...

Let's read the verses together in their full context so you can get a feel for the greatness of God's master plan. *Then Melchizedek king of Salem brought out bread and wine. He was priest of God Most High, and he blessed Abram, saying, "Blessed be Abram by God Most High, Creator of heaven and earth. And praise be to God Most High, who delivered your enemies into your hand". Then Abram gave him **a tenth** (maaser) of everything. The king of Sodom said to Abram, Give me the people and keep the goods for yourself. But Abram said to the king of Sodom: With raised hand I have sworn an oath to the LORD, God Most High, Creator of heaven and earth, that I will accept nothing belonging to you, not even a thread or the strap of a sandal, so that you will never be able to say, 'I made Abram **rich** (aser).' I will accept nothing but what my men have eaten and the share that belongs to the men who went with me - to Aner, Eshkol and Mamre. Let them have their share.*

The second scripture on the subject of tithing is found in the well-known and often quoted Malachi 3:10-12. It reads: *"Bring the whole tithe into the storehouse, so that there may be food in My house, and test Me now in this," says the LORD of hosts, "if I will not open for you the windows of heaven and **pour out for you a blessing until it overflows**. Then I will **rebuke the devourer for you**, so that it will not destroy the fruits of the ground; nor will your vine in the field cast its grapes, says the LORD of hosts. All the nations will call you blessed, for you shall be a delightful land'.* I doubt that further explanation is needed here!

Many churches present the law of sowing and reaping - giving our tithes and offerings - in a way that leaves a negative aftertaste. We are called to give in order to receive, yet are seldom instructed on the principles and depth of the act.

Our lack of understanding in this area sometimes makes us feel that tithes and offerings are a way to try and twist God's arm, as if we're trying to force Him to do something that He doesn't particularly want to do. As a result of this, we feel guilty and uneasy in our hearts. This in turn totally keeps us from boldly asking God for the things that we need and desire, resulting in deficiency and frustration. The whole concept of what God intended for our blessing and provision is then lost. Do not allow this to be the case with you.

I hope to have shown you in this chapter that obtaining provision in this awesome way is entirely God's idea. It is a heavenly and well-thought out plan to give His children provision and abundance. Do not ever forget that provision is part of your salvation, an expression of God's extravagant love for you.

Now that you know this, don't you dare push His blessings aside. Don't you dare reject what God has sent you through the death of His Son! Boldly stand and take hold of what Has been so freely and lovingly offered to you. Your Heavenly Father longs to see you thrive in your personal life, the Kingdom Way!

You now understand that struggling for provision is a choice you really don't need to be making anymore. Available to you from this moment forward is the opportunity to focus on your purpose. That is what the next chapter is about.

Focus points and tips for success on my journey to personal thriving, the Kingdom Way:

- I continuously and eagerly look for ways to give my offerings. I now know that every time I give, I free myself from the earth-cursed way of obtaining provision.
- I relentlessly give my tithes. Each time I do, I believe that God Himself rebukes the devourer on my behalf.

Practical reflection and consideration ('My Purpose'): How will your understanding of the blessings of giving your tithes and offerings make you more of a cheerful giver? What is your 'little bit' that you can give God to work with on your behalf?

Give an offering/sow some money at least one time this week, according to the principles you've learned. What is your heart disposition now in comparison to the last time you sowed? How did it feel to release your faith for your provision? Were there still old lies or feelings of guilt to conquer?

By doing this exercise I learned about myself that:

_____

_____

_____

_____

_____

_____

_____

_____

_____

_____

_____

_____

_____

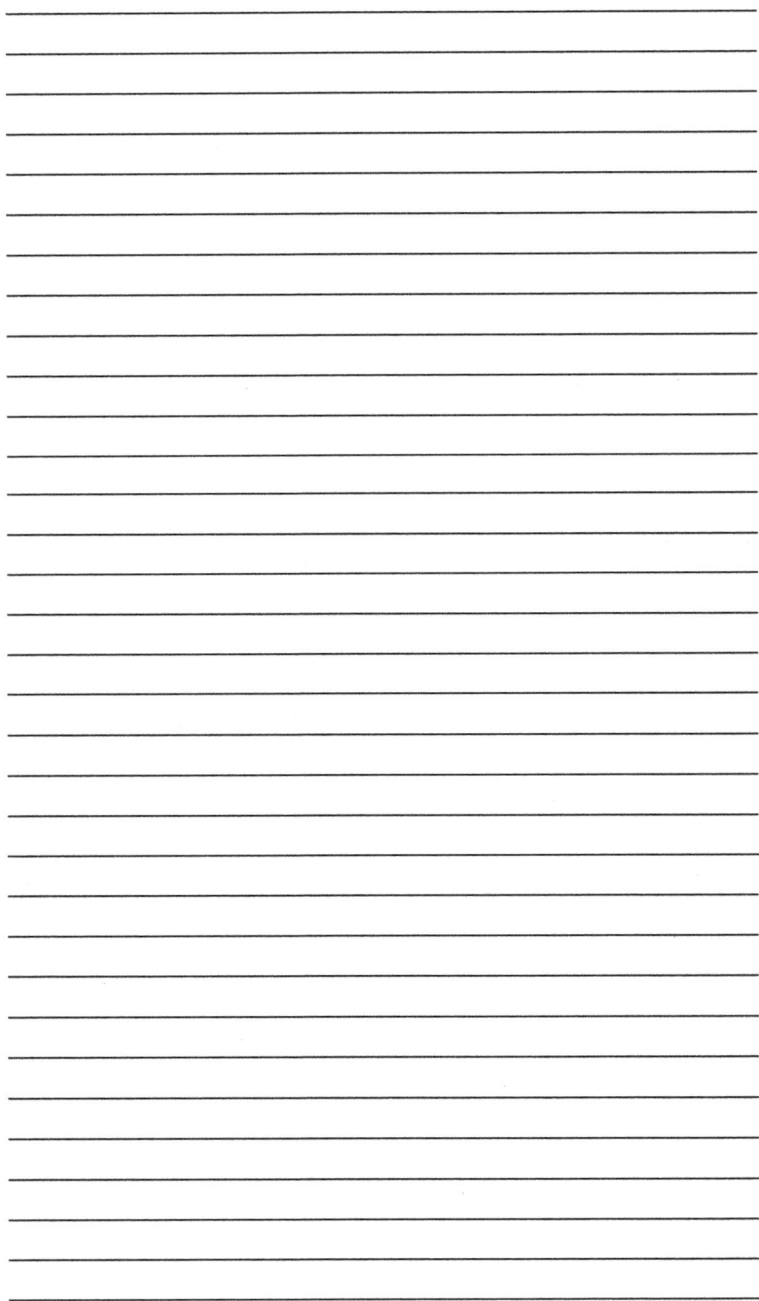

CHAPTER 13
My Unique Purpose in Life

Purpose: In this chapter you will discover your personal purpose through which God can keep a continual stream of blessing and provision flowing into your life.

You now understand that you are called to live free from hoarding and running after the things of this world for provision. I therefore challenge you to believe God's laws and find ways to regularly sow money into the Kingdom of Heaven. You are now set free from the burden of doing it the 'worlds way'. What a difference this will make in the way you can approach your purpose, right? Knowing that all else is already taken care of, let's take a look at what your specific purpose is all about!

Finding your purpose will give you the greatest satisfaction in life. One of the things you will need to understand firsthand is that your purpose is never about you. [14] It will always be about promoting the glory of the Kingdom of Heaven. It will always be about service to others. God's highest purpose for your life is to love God and to love others as yourself!

Purpose is all about using the good, the bad, and the ugly things in your life as a rich and colorful foundation upon which others can steadily build their lives. It's about sharing who you are and what you've been through to elevate and inspire others. You help others to transcend, to do better, and to become better people. Purpose is about sharing the hopes and dreams that God has placed in your heart with a world in need - a world looking for hope and (yes!) purpose.

What is equally important for you to know is that you have already been ordained and fully equipped for your purpose. You already have everything you need inside of you to do what you are called to do! Once you put the pieces together and begin to walk in your purpose and destiny, you no longer merely exist. You feel alive, passionate and driven!

There are often several traits that stand out in a person's life. There is so much in which we find joy and excel. But in each person there are at least one or two qualities or experiences that really stand out. Those are the very things that we can share with others to make their learning curve shorter and get them to where they're going faster. It can seem confusing and overwhelming to try and discover your true reason for living - that one thing on which you should focus.

I want to present to you eight questions that will quickly get you on your way to knowing your reason for being. Let's look at these and then I will propose the most useful way to answer them.

Discovering your purpose in life - 8 questions

Let's get an idea now about what you are passionate. What makes you smile? What are you good at? What gives you positive energy just thinking about it? What have you learned along life's journey that you are burning to share with the world? What could you do for hours on end, even if you never got paid for it? That is your passion, that is your destiny, and that is your purpose in life! The purpose questions I share with you here are divided into four categories - your abilities, your experiences, your opportunities and your passions. Here they are:

My Abilities:
1. What are my abilities and/or spiritual gifts?
2. What type of training or schooling have I received over the course of the years that can be used to benefit others?

My Experiences:
3. What lessons have I learned from my past mistakes?
4. What are some negative things people have inflicted upon me that God can use to help others?

My Opportunities:
5. What are some unique people and/or opportunities that have shaped or have benefitted me?
6. What is unique about me (education, experience, looks, anything else...)?

My Passions:
7. What am I always excited to talk to others about?
8. If money was no issue (and by this time, it shouldn't be anymore), what would I spend my time doing?

How to go about answering the purpose questions
Begin now to answer the above questions for yourself. You can best answer them by using key words rather than full sentences. For example:
Question Number 1: 'What are my abilities and/or spiritual gifts?' Possible answer: singing, public speaking, etc.
Question Number 2: 'What type of training or schooling have I received over the course of the years that can be used to benefit others?' Possible answer: In college - social work, helped children in their development. Swimming instructor - gave swimming lessons.

Question Number 5: 'What are some unique people and/or opportunities that have shaped me or that have benefitted me by what they imparted to me?' Possible answer: Coach - taught me to never give up. Grandmother - taught me to always be patient with everyone.

Okay, I think you get the idea. Continue down the line answering each question in this same way. Take time and begin immediately.

After that, put your answers together in 'essay form', beginning your sentences with: 'My purpose in life is to....' Let your heart lead you in connecting your different abilities, experiences, opportunities and passions and see what you come up with. You may be surprised when you see the things that were in your heart for years now suddenly become crystal clear on paper. It can be a magical moment. I know it was for me...

My own personal purpose essay
I want to share my own personal essay with you, based on the answers to my purpose questions. Here it is:

My purpose in life is to use my public speaking abilities to clearly convey spiritual truths, teaching people that:
- Knowing God's truths and putting His Word above their emotions and circumstances make that Truth become visible in their life; and
- Learning to see as God sees will make life actually become what He says it should be (Kingdom living).

I use my ability to make people feel 'seen' and appreciated during my coaching sessions to let them realize:
- The importance of being accountable to someone who cares and hears God's voice; and
- The benefits of having someone speak truth to them even

though it hurts and even though that is not what they want to hear at that moment.

I share my personal testimony of how I was ultimately able to joyfully trust God because of believing in His faithfulness, because faith always works! My purpose is also to bless people by sharing my testimony and my books on radio, television, in churches, in public places, through the internet and on the streets. I allow God to use my calm, confident, and peaceful spirit to draw people to what I have to say. As a result they are touched, transformed, and healed. Knowing my purpose has given me clear direction and allowed me to prioritize my activities in order to begin living out the life that God has intended for me!

Steps to begin walking out your purpose and destiny

1. Once you have a draft of your purpose essay ready, write or print it on a sheet of paper. Read and meditate on it daily and begin to actually see yourself fulfilling it. How does it feel, look, sound to be fully living out your purpose without having to deal with the burden of provision? Now that's a fulfilling life, right? This is what the Kingdom of Heaven intended for you!

You can also turn your completed purpose essay into a visual tool and use it as a basis for meditation. I will briefly comment on this in the chapter dealing with 'visualizing your destiny'.

2. Choose and perform your first 3 action steps toward your purpose in the first week of completing your essay. No matter how small the steps you make, get moving immediately! You may call or e-mail someone for some information. You may begin writing the first few sentences of your e-book. You may begin assembling your prototype for that idea you have... Whatever it is, get moving!

You will notice that as soon as you do, your zest for life is activated and you become totally excited about who you are called to be! That, my friend, is the Kingdom Way!

3. Find a good friend, teacher, parents, or anyone else that you trust to be your accountability partner. Meet with him or her on a weekly or biweekly basis. Share what you have done so far and receive direction toward making further steps. Discuss any roadblocks you may face. Commit to keep moving forward! I am getting excited just sharing this with you. I hope you are too!

After you find your purpose in life, it is highly recommendable that you have Kingdom character and the integrity to sustain it. This way you are sure to bring continued glory to your Heavenly Father. In the next chapter we will look at ways to develop and maintain Godly character.

Focus points and tips for success on my journey to personal thriving, the Kingdom Way:

- I am keenly aware that my highest purpose is to love God and love people. My purpose in life is never about me.
- I immediately begin taking steps to fulfill my purpose, no matter how small.

Practical reflection and consideration ('My Purpose'): After answering your purpose questions, what is the very first step you can take to fulfill your destiny? Think about who can function as your accountability partner. Immediately call that person and share with him or her your plan to begin living your purpose.

By doing this exercise I learned about myself that:

_____

_____

_____

_____

_____

_____

_____

_____

_____

_____

_____

_____

_____

_____

_____

_____

_____

_____

PART 6
MY LIFESTYLE
Golden Nuggets for a Life of Success and Thriving

CHAPTER 14
Taking Responsibility for My Lifestyle

Purpose: In this chapter you will learn how to maintain your personal responsibility for a successful and thriving lifestyle.

Lifestyle [15] is described as: the way in which a person lives.
For me, the word lifestyle denotes a sense of personal responsibility. Your lifestyle is not something into which you are necessarily born. It is largely determined by the choices you make for the quality and direction of your life.

If this is true, there are some critical questions that we need to be asking ourselves throughout our life journey. Questions like: What does my life look like? Am I enjoying who I am in Christ? Does my life reflect the blessings and glory of the Kingdom of Heaven? Is my life similar to or in worse shape than people operating under the kingdom of this world? Does my life remain unchanged year after year? Do I see little or no progress at all in my personal life? Am I still stifled and challenged by the things people do to me? Am I still traumatized by past whisperings of the devil or others? Am I experiencing continual strife and difficulty in my dealings with man?

Remember that as a child of the Kingdom of Heaven your identity reads as follows: **you are who God says you are, you have what God says you have, and you can do what God says you can do**. You have heard this truth many times throughout this book. I believe it is crucial that you speak it to yourself regularly. It is the absolute foundation upon which you can live a life of continual thriving and success, the Kingdom Way! There's no reason for your life to be merely a dim reflection of the Kingdom of Heaven. Why should it? You have already been given every spiritual blessing in Christ and all things pertaining to life and godliness (Eph. 1:3, 2 Peter 1:3).

This last truth should also become more and more evident to you as we proceed through this book. Conversely, we must also continue to accept that God can never be blamed for our lack of thriving in life, since we know He is never indifferent and always willing to help us.

I believe that much of our lack of success and thriving in life is because we do not actively incorporate the Kingdom Way into our personal lifestyle. We allow our own personal interpretations and opinions to be exalted above God's. We allow our circumstances and negative experiences to reign supreme over and above the truth of the Kingdom of Heaven.

This chapter may be quite confrontational. It is intended to be so. Why? Because if you've come this far in this book you are now at a place where you can assertively make a decision for or against God. By now you have read enough to be able to decide whether or not the God exhibited in this book is One you want to follow and to whom you wholly give your life. Throughout this book, He has been presented to you in a real way. You have read about His overwhelming and untiring love for you - an amazing love that had Him give His all so that we could access the Kingdom of Heaven.

Can you see the beauty of this? Can you accept this love? Do you understand the depth of it? If you do, you should by now be capable of making a decision based on who He is. You should also have the desire to lead a lifestyle fit for a child of the Kingdom of Heaven.

To further your commitment to a Heavenly lifestyle, I want to present to you two Kingdom Life truths to reflect on and live by. These truths will help you take personal responsibility for your lifestyle. Again, this will be confronting, but I'm glad to say that these are all God's words, not mine.

We find the first Kingdom Life Truth in **Matthew 7:21:** *"Not everyone **who says to me**, 'Lord, Lord,' will enter the kingdom of heaven, but only the one **who does the will of my Father** who is in heaven".* Are we doing the will of God? I know we often quote it, talk about it, listen to it, sing about it, but do we also live it? As long as we do not, our life remains powerless and void of any manifestation of the Kingdom of Heaven. We continue to miss out on the 'supernatural-normal' life that is destined for every Kingdom child. The first truth: Be a doer of the Word. [16]

The second Kingdom Life Truth is found in **Colossians 3:2** where it says: ***Set your minds** on **things above**, not on earthly things.* How much time do you spend on earthly things such as: watching television, listening to worldly music, surfing the internet, engaging in social media, reading newspapers, magazines, and novels, talking on the phone about trivialities? Is the time spent on these earthly things more extensive than time spent on living in the truths of the Kingdom of Heaven? If so, the mediocrity of this world will become your norm. While the things of this world begin to seem more and more normal to you, the life-giving truths of the Kingdom will appear foreign, and even unattractive.

Based on all that we have now learned about the Kingdom of Heaven, the kingdom of this world is a very sad place to be, won't you agree? When we occupy ourselves with earthly things we miss out on the abundant blessings from the Kingdom to which we truly belong - the Heavenly Kingdom.

I want to talk to you now about some key areas in which we can take responsibility for a Kingdom lifestyle of success and thriving. These are:

1. Responsibility for **(a) enduring hardships and (b) living a life of integrity** as the Kingdom Way for success in our personal life;
2. Responsibility for **communicating effectively** as the Kingdom Way for success in our relationships; and
3. Responsibility for **using our time wisely** as the Kingdom Way for success in our spiritual life.

1(a) Taking responsibility for enduring hardships in difficult times, the Kingdom Way.

Endurance [17] is the ability to suffer patiently in an unpleasant or difficult process or situation without giving way. Even though Jesus was the Son of God, life on earth certainly was not without challenges. His very reason for being on earth 'invited' challenges, disappointments, hardships and the need to make tough but necessary decisions. We, too, will continually face challenges in this life. How should our attitude be in these times?

Let's take a look at Jesus' lessons on endurance.

How do you endure dealing with hardships? Answer: By never walking away from responsibility or tough circumstances, but by facing them through prayer - alone or with a group of close friends. Praying helps you develop personal resolve to do the hard tasks that need to be done. *Then cometh Jesus with them unto a place called Gethsemane, and saith unto the disciples, Sit ye here, while I go and pray yonder. And he took with him Peter and the two sons of Zebedee, and began to be sorrowful and very heavy. Then saith he unto them, My soul is exceeding sorrowful, even unto death: tarry ye here, and watch with me. And he went a little farther, and fell on his face, and prayed, saying, O my Father, if it be possible, let this cup pass from me: nevertheless not as I will, but as thou wilt. And he cometh unto the disciples, and findeth them asleep, and saith unto Peter, What, could ye not watch with me one hour? Watch and pray, that ye enter not into temptation: the spirit indeed is willing, but the flesh is weak.He went away again the second time, and prayed, saying, O my Father, if this cup may not pass away from me, except I drink it, thy will be done. And he came and found them asleep again: for their eyes were heavy. And he left them, and went away again, and prayed the third time, saying the same words* (Matt. 26:36-44).

Unfortunately Jesus' friends fell asleep on Him and left Him to pray by Himself in His most difficult time of suffering. I hope that in your case your friends will be always there to prayerfully support you.

How do you endure dealing with betrayal and injustice? Answer: Through exercising the power of forgiveness. Jesus shows us how forgiveness and compassion intersect, when He prayed for the Father's forgiveness. *Father forgive them, for they know not what they do* (Luke 23:34). People act unjustly and harshly when they are not experiencing God in some particular area of their life. Realizing this will make us better able to forgive and be compassionate toward others.

How do you endure dealing with personal failures, especially if it's your own fault? Answer: By receiving Jesus' forgiveness. His forgiveness enables you to forgive yourself and move on. *And the scribes and Pharisees brought unto him a woman taken in adultery; and when they had set her in the midst, they say unto him, Master, this woman was taken in adultery, in the very act. Now Moses in the law commanded us, that such should be stoned: but what sayest thou? This they said, tempting him, that they might have to accuse him. But Jesus stooped down, and with his finger wrote on the ground, as though he heard them not. So when they continued asking him, he lifted up himself, and said unto them, He that is without sin among you, let him first cast a stone at her.*

And again he stooped down, and wrote on the ground. And they which heard it, being convicted by their own conscience, went out one by one, beginning at the eldest, even unto the last: and Jesus was left alone, and the woman standing in the midst. When Jesus had lifted up himself, and saw none but the woman, he said unto her, Woman, where are those thine accusers? hath no man condemned thee? She said, No man, Lord. And Jesus said unto her, Neither do I condemn thee: go, and sin no more (John 8:3-11).

When we become overwhelmed by Jesus' goodness and nonjudgmental attitude towards us, it gives us the power to 'go and sin no more'.

How do you endure having to prepare for big, important decisions? Answer: By taking time to pray to the Father for wisdom. Jesus spent the night in prayer which brought clarity in His decision making. So must we. *And it came to pass in those days, that he went out into a mountain to pray, and continued all night in prayer to God. And when it was day, he called unto him* *his disciples: and of them he chose twelve, whom also he named apostles* (Luke 6:12-13).

1(b) Living a life of integrity, the Kingdom Way.

Integrity[18] is the quality of being honest and having strong moral principles. Jesus came to represent The Kingdom of Heaven as a new way of living. He often met with conflict because people had difficulty accepting this new way. In spite of that, His morality and standards remained anchored in the truths of the Kingdom of Heaven.

Let's see what we can learn from Jesus on the topic of integrity.

How do you show integrity in the midst of opposition? Answer: By always speaking truth and doing what's right in spite of the possibility of conflict. Always stand up for what you believe, no matter what others may think. *Woe unto you, scribes and Pharisees, hypocrites! for ye are like unto whited sepulchres, which indeed appear beautiful outward, but are within full of dead men's bones, and of all uncleanness. Even so ye also outwardly appear righteous unto men, but within ye are full of hypocrisy and iniquity* (Matt. 23:27-28).

Jesus was especially honest and direct to those who spoke the right words but did not live it (the hypocrites). He was always straightforward but never disrespectful.

How do you show integrity in spite of what other's think you should say or do? Answer: By always seeking God's approval and not that of man, and by letting obedience to the Kingdom of Heaven be your only internal anchor. *And Jesus entered and passed through Jericho. And, behold, there was a man named Zacchaeus, which was the chief among the publicans, and he was rich. And he sought to see Jesus who he was; and could not for* the press, because he was little of stature. And he ran before, and climbed up into a sycamore tree to see him: for he was to pass that way. And when Jesus came to the place, he looked up, and saw him, and said unto him, Zacchaeus, make haste, and come down; for today I must abide at thy house. And he made haste, and came down, and received him joyfully. And when they saw it, they all murmured, saying, That he was gone to be guest with a man that is a sinner.

And Zacchaeus stood, and said unto the Lord: Behold, Lord, the half of my goods I give to the poor; and if I have taken anything from any man by false accusation, I restore him fourfold. And Jesus said unto him, This day is salvation come to this house, forsomuch as he also is a son of Abraham. For the Son of man is come to seek and to save that which was lost (Luke 19:1-10).

How do you maintain integrity when there seems to be an 'illegal' easy way out? Answer: By knowing your mission and purpose in life. This way you can easily recognize the temptations that are sent to distract you from fulfilling your purpose.

Then was Jesus led up of the Spirit into the wilderness to be tempted of the devil. And when he had fasted forty days and forty nights, he was afterward an hungred. And when the tempter came to him, he said, If thou be the Son of God, command that these stones be made bread. But he answered and said, It is written, Man shall not live by bread alone, but by every word that proceedeth out of the mouth of God.

Then the devil taketh him up into the holy city, And setteth him on a pinnacle of the temple, And saith unto him, If thou be the Son of God, cast thyself down: for it is written, He shall give his angels charge concerning thee: and in their hands they shall bear thee up, lest at any time thou dash thy foot against a stone. Jesus said unto him, It is written again, Thou shalt not tempt the Lord thy God.

Again, the devil taketh him up into an exceeding high mountain, and sheweth him all the kingdoms of the world, and the glory of them; And saith unto him, All these things will I give thee, if thou wilt fall down and worship me. Then saith Jesus unto him, Get thee hence, Satan: for it is written, Thou shalt worship the Lord thy God, and him only shalt thou serve. Then the devil leaveth him, and, behold, angels came and ministered unto him (Matt. 4:1-11).

Jesus knew He was called to the cross to bring salvation to all mankind. When the devil tempted Him, He did not relent. Jesus did not accept the temptation to worship the devil as a way to avoid having to go to the cross.

How do you show integrity when having to accomplish a tough task? Answer: By finishing what you start and not giving up before time. Completing the task set before you brings glory, joy, and a feeling of fulfillment. It also makes you credible in the eyes of others. *"I have glorified thee on the earth: I have finished the work which thou gavest me to do. And now, O Father, glorify thou me with thine own self with the glory which I had with thee before the world was. I have manifested thy name unto the men which thou gavest me out of the world: thine they were, and thou gavest them me; and they have kept thy word. Now they have known that all things whatsoever thou hast given me are of thee"* (John 17:4-7).

So, persevere and finish well.

2. Taking responsibility for effective communication, the Kingdom Way.
Communication[19] is the imparting or exchanging of information by speaking, writing, or using some other medium. Effective communication involves talking, listening, making eye contact, using your body language, allowing pauses for reflection, and asking questions. Jesus was a master communicator.

Here's what Jesus' style of communicating teaches us.

How do you communicate effectively to people in need?
Answer: By being a person of compassion. People in the world need answers. A compassionate attitude helps us provide this to them. Once we approach others with compassion, the way we view them and their circumstances changes. *And Jesus, when he came out, saw much people, and was moved with compassion toward them, because they were as sheep not having a shepherd: and he began to teach them many things* (Mark 6:34).

Compassion leads to action. *And Jesus went forth, and saw a great multitude, and was moved with compassion toward them, and he healed their sick* (Matt. 14:14).

Compassion seeks solutions. *Then Jesus called his disciples unto him, and said, I have compassion on the multitude, because they continue with me now three days, and have nothing to eat: and I will not send them away fasting, lest they faint in the way. And his disciples say unto him, Whence should we have so much bread in the wilderness, as to fill so great a multitude? And Jesus saith unto them, How many loaves have ye? And they said, Seven, and a few little fishes. And he commanded the multitude to sit down on the ground. And he took the seven loaves and the fishes, and gave thanks, and brake them, and gave to his disciples, and the disciples to the multitude. And they did all eat, and were filled: and they took up of the broken meat that was left seven baskets full. And they that did eat were four thousand men, beside women and children. And he sent away the multitude, and took ship, and came into the coasts of Magdala* (Matt. 15:32-39).

Compassion speaks straight to the heart of man. *Then Jesus beholding him loved him, and said unto him, One thing thou lackest: go thy way, sell whatsoever thou hast, and give to the poor, and thou shalt have treasure in heaven: and come, take up the cross, and follow me. And he was sad at that saying, and went away grieved: for he had great possessions* (Mark 10:21-22).

How do you communicate effectively with people who are rejected? Answer: By acknowledging them and making them feel 'seen'. *Doing this causes them to (re)gain dignity in their own eyes and the eyes of others. Acknowledging people can also lead to their personal restoration. And they came to Jericho: and as he went out of Jericho with his disciples and a great number of people, blind Bartimaeus, the son of Timaeus, sat by the highway side begging. And when he heard that it was Jesus of Nazareth, he began to cry out, and say, Jesus, thou son of David, have mercy on me. And many charged him that he should hold his peace: but he cried the more a great deal, Thou son of David, have mercy on me. And Jesus stood still, and commanded him to be called.*

And they call the blind man, saying unto him, Be of good comfort, rise; he calleth thee. And he, casting away his garment, rose, and came to Jesus. And Jesus answered and said unto him, What wilt thou that I should do unto thee? The blind man said unto him, Lord, that I might receive my sight. And Jesus said unto him, Go thy way; thy faith hath made thee whole. And immediately he received his sight, and followed Jesus in the way (Mark 10:46-52).

How do you communicate effectively with those who feel as if their situation is desperate and hopeless? Answer: By using the art of silence, allowing their heart to be revealed, and by allowing them to express themselves and receive answers. *Then Jesus went thence, and departed into the coasts of Tyre and Sidon. And, behold, a woman of Canaan came out of the same coasts, and cried unto him, saying, Have mercy on me, O Lord, thou son of David; my daughter is grievously vexed with a devil. But he answered her not a word. And his disciples came and besought him, saying, Send her away; for she crieth after us.*

But he answered and said, I am not sent but unto the lost sheep of the house of Israel. Then came she and worshipped him, saying, Lord, help me. But he answered and said, It is not meet to take the children's bread, and to cast it to dogs. And she said, Truth, Lord: yet the dogs eat of the crumbs which fall from their masters' table. Then Jesus answered and said unto her, O woman, great is thy faith: be it unto thee even as thou wilt. And her daughter was made whole from that very hour (Matt. 15:21-28).

How do you communicate effectively with those who are afraid to expect anything good from life? Answer: By asking questions even when you already know the answer. This creates a feeling of safety. When people feel cared for and safe, they open up their heart. That is when they reveal their true self and are able to ask for what they really need and desire. *Jesus stopped and said, "Call him." So they called to the blind man, "Cheer up! On your feet! He's calling you." Throwing his cloak aside, he jumped to his feet and came to Jesus. "What do you want me to do for you?" Jesus asked him. The blind man said, "Rabbi, I want to see." "Go," said Jesus, "your faith has healed you." Immediately he received his sight and followed Jesus along the road* (Mark 10:49-52).

3. Taking responsibility for using time, the Kingdom Way.
Time[20] is the continued progress of existence as affecting people and things. Jesus said that without Him we can do nothing (John 15:5). If all we give to God is the scraps of our time, we should not be surprised when we do not experience a life of abundance.

Here are the lessons Jesus teaches us about using our time wisely.

How do you use time well in the first hours of the day? Answer: By resting with Jesus. Every day, make it a conscious habit to spend time alone communing with Him.[21] Preferably in the quiet, early morning hours. That is the time when Jesus is most easily 'found'. *After these things Jesus shewed himself again to the disciples at the sea of Tiberias; and on this wise shewed he himself. There were together Simon Peter, and Thomas called Didymus, and Nathanael of Cana in Galilee, and the sons of Zebedee, and two other of his disciples. Simon Peter saith unto them, I go a fishing. They say unto him, We also go with thee.*

They went forth, and entered into a ship immediately; and that night they caught nothing. But when the morning was now come, Jesus stood on the shore: but the disciples knew not that it was Jesus. Then Jesus saith unto them, Children, have ye any meat? They answered him, No. And he said unto them, Cast the net on the right side of the ship, and ye shall find. They cast therefore, and now they were not able to draw it for the multitude of fishes. Therefore that disciple whom Jesus loved saith unto Peter, It is the Lord. Now when Simon Peter heard that it was the Lord, he girt his fisher's coat unto him, (for he was naked,) and did cast himself into the sea. And the other disciples came in a little ship; (for they were not far from land, but as it were two hundred cubits,) dragging the net with fishes. As soon then as they were come to land, they saw a fire of coals there, and fish laid thereon, and bread.

Jesus saith unto them, Bring of the fish which ye have now caught. Simon Peter went up and drew the net to land full of great fishes, an hundred and fifty and three: and for all there were so many, yet was not the net broken. Jesus saith unto them, Come and dine. And none of the disciples durst ask him, Who art thou? knowing that it was the Lord. Jesus then cometh, and taketh bread, and giveth them, and fish likewise (John 21:1-13). And also: *And in the morning, rising up a great while before day, he went out, and departed into a solitary place, and there prayed* (Mark 1:35).

How do you use time when the activities of your day are hectic and somewhat overwhelming? Answer: By making a conscious effort to pull yourself out of the busy-ness of your day and connect with Jesus. You can listen to a message, read the Bible or any other spiritually uplifting Christian book. *Now it came to pass, as they went, that he entered into a certain village: and a certain woman named Martha received him into her house. And she had a sister called Mary, which also sat at Jesus' feet, and heard his word. But Martha was cumbered about much serving, and came to him, and said, Lord, dost thou not care that my sister hath left me to serve alone? bid her therefore that she help me. And Jesus answered and said unto her, Martha, Martha, thou art careful and troubled about many things: But one thing is needful: and Mary hath chosen that good part, which shall not be taken away from her* (Luke 10:38-42).

The life of Jesus and His disciples shows us that once the chaos of the day begins, it's hard to pull away to spend time alone with Him. This suggests that the early morning hours still really are the most effective. *And he called unto him the twelve, and began to send them forth by two and two; and gave them power over unclean spirits; And commanded them that they should take nothing for their journey, save a staff only; no scrip, no bread, no money in their purse: But be shod with sandals; and not put on two coats. And he said unto them, In what place soever ye enter into an house, there abide till ye depart from that place. And whosoever shall not receive you, nor hear you, when ye depart thence, shake off the dust under your feet for a testimony against them. Verily I say unto you, It shall be more tolerable for Sodom and Gomorrha in the day of judgment, than for that city. And they went out, and preached that men should repent. And they cast out many devils, and anointed with oil many that were sick, and healed them [...]*

And the apostles gathered themselves together unto Jesus, and told him all things, both what they had done, and what they had taught. And he said unto them, Come ye yourselves apart into a desert place, and rest a while: for there were many coming and going, and they had no leisure so much as to eat. And they departed into a desert place by ship privately. And the people saw them departing, and many knew him, and ran afoot thither out of all cities, and outwent them, and came together unto him (Mark 6:7-13, 30-33).

How do you use time when in the outdoors? Answer: By seeing and noticing nature and casually learning life lessons from it (about the sparrow, the lilies, the mountains...). Being in the outdoors reminds us of the greatness of God and helps us to objectively evaluate and rethink our perspective on life. By watching nature in all its beauty we also become more aware of the Father's care for us.

"Are not two sparrows sold for a penny? Yet not one of them will fall to the ground outside your Father's care. And even the very hairs of your head are all numbered. So don't be afraid; you are worth more than many sparrows (Matt. 10:29-31). Also: 'And why do you worry about clothes? See how the flowers of the field grow. They do not labor or spin. Yet I tell you that not even Solomon in all his splendor was dressed like one of these. If that is how God clothes the grass of the field, which is here today and tomorrow is thrown into the fire, will he not much more clothe you—you of little faith? So do not worry, saying, 'What shall we eat?' or 'What shall we drink?' or 'What shall we wear?'"(Matt. 6:28-31). And: "Have faith in God," Jesus answered. "Truly I tell you, if anyone says to this mountain, 'Go, throw yourself into the sea,' and does not doubt in their heart but believes that what they say will happen, it will be done for them. Therefore I tell you, whatever you ask for in prayer, believe that you have received it, and it will be yours" (Mark 11:22-24).

How do you use time noticing what's important in life? Answer: By living in the moment and being 'present'. Let's not be constantly focused on the 'next thing' that needs to be done. Enjoy and have awareness of who you are and where you are in the 'now'. In spite of all that needed to be done, Jesus was always focused and fully consumed by the task at hand. He was always 'about people'. He took time for each one individually, and so should we in our daily life. *Soon afterward, Jesus went to a town called Nain, and his disciples and a large crowd went along with him. As he approached the town gate, a dead person was being carried out—the only son of his mother, and she was a widow. And a large crowd from the town was with her. When the Lord saw her, his heart went out to her and he said, "Don't cry." Then he went up and touched the bier they were carrying him on, and the bearers stood still. He said, 'Young man, I say to you, get up!'*

The dead man sat up and began to talk, and Jesus gave him back to his mother. They were all filled with awe and praised God. 'A great prophet has appeared among us, they said. 'God has come to help his people. This news about Jesus spread throughout Judea and the surrounding country (Luke 7:11-17).

How do you most effectively use time to fulfill your purpose?
Answer: By delegating authority, equipping people and giving clear working instructions. Delegating frees you up so you can focus on your prime purpose in life. *After this the Lord appointed seventy-two others and sent them two by two ahead of him to every town and place where he was about to go. He told them, "The harvest is plentiful, but the workers are few.* **Ask the Lord** *of the harvest, therefore, to send out workers into his harvest field. Go! I am sending you out like lambs among wolves.* **Do not take** *a purse or bag or sandals; and do not greet anyone on the road.* **When you enter a house, first say,** *'Peace to this house.' If someone who promotes peace is there, your peace will rest on them; if not, it will return to you.* **Stay there, eating and drinking** *whatever they give you, for the worker deserves his wages.* **Do not move around** *from*

house to house. When you enter a town and are welcomed, eat what is offered to you. **Heal the sick** *who are there and tell them, 'The kingdom of God has come near to you.' But* **when you enter a town and are not welcomed, go into its streets and say,** *'Even the dust of your town we wipe from our feet as a warning to you. Yet be sure of this: The kingdom of God has come near.' I tell you, it will be more bearable on that day for Sodom than for that town"* (Luke 10:1-12).

How do you use time preparing others to leave a legacy? Answer: By not feeling intimidated, but rather empowered, by others who know and accomplish more than you will. *"Verily, verily, I say unto you, He that believeth on me, the works that I do shall he do also; and greater works than these shall he do; because I go unto my Father"* (John 14:12). Consequently, let us not be people who hoard knowledge and information. Do not strive to be the only expert in any given area. Share your expertise. This will increase your own personal growth. If Jesus had no fear empowering us in this way, why should we?

I hope you can see your own personal identity clearly revealed in the previous paragraphs. You know why? Because if you have put on the life of Christ, what you see in Him is who you are! Simply beholding Christ's life allows you to become who you already are in Him. Yes, you will actually see God's quality and way of life becoming more and more evident in your life. Not by forcing it, but simply by beholding Him.

The Bible teaches us that we become like Him by beholding Him. *And we all, who with unveiled faces contemplate the Lord's glory, are being transformed into his image with ever-increasing glory, which comes from the Lord, who is the Spirit* (2 Corinthians 3:18). And: *By this, love is perfected with us, so that we may have confidence in the day of judgment; because as He is, so also are we in this world* (1 John 4:17). Please, take time to meditate on the above Bible verses and see yourself through the eyes of the finished work of Christ. Don't struggle, just simply 'be'!

In the next chapter we will focus deeper on the idea of becoming what you behold. We will talk about visualization as a way to transform into and experience that which you want to see in your life.

Focus points and tips for success on my journey to personal thriving, the Kingdom Way:

- I take full responsibility for my lifestyle and choices. I live a life worthy of the Kingdom to which I belong.
- I continually look to Jesus and the way He lived life, for I become like Him by beholding Him.

Practical reflection and consideration ('My Lifestyle'): Take a critical look at your average day. What do you spend most of your time doing? What are the results of your choices? What changes are you willing to make in your day in order to have more time communing with Jesus?

By doing this exercise I learned about myself that:

_____

_____

_____

_____

_____

_____

_____

_____

_____

_____

_____

_____

_____

_____

_____

_____

_____

_____

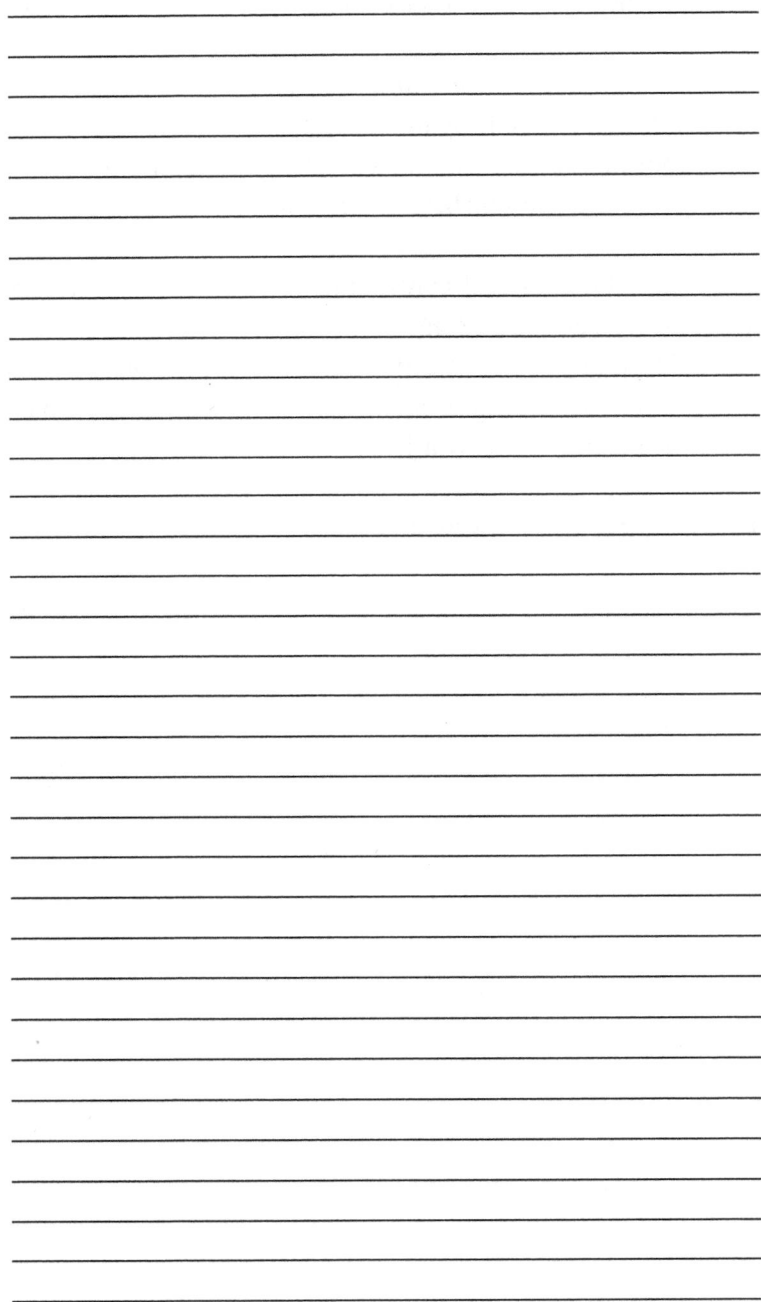

CHAPTER 15
Practical 'Time-Tips' and Visualizing My Destiny

Purpose: In this chapter you will learn to develop your own personal visualization aids so you can begin to experience a life of success and growth today!

In the previous chapter we looked at some practical ways to develop in ourselves the character of Christ and align our life with the Kingdom of Heaven. I now want to add some practical tips for eliminating time-wasters so that you can use your time more efficiently. These simple tips can serve as useful tools of empowerment in your journey of thriving and not just surviving in your personal life. They are basic, practical, and hopefully very useful to you. Here they are:

- Make it a habit to wake up at least 30 minutes earlier than your usual time to be alone with Jesus. Read, worship, listen to a sermon or just sit and realize that He is there. Listen to how He prepares and equips you for the day ahead.

- When your alarm goes off in the morning, apply the 5 second rule. Get up and out of your warm and comfy bed within 5 seconds of hearing the alarm signal. No excuses, no procrastination! How you spend the first few moments of your day is crucial. Don't allow yourself to get off to a grumpy start because you don't get up on time.

- Make use of your God-given 'expressions of worship' several times during the day: Lift up your hands in worship to God, sing songs of worship either out loud or under your breath, speak in tongues, pray regularly. If the circumstances permit, do these expressions while gently rocking your body from side to side. Either close your eyes or have them rolled upward toward heaven. Sound funny? It may. But all these postures and attitudes of worship have been given by God. They help slow down your brainwaves from the 'rush and chaos' of everyday life. They will make your heart receptive and more able to connect to God's Truths and directions.

- Never waste the idle moments in your day. When you have to wait your turn or stand in line, always take an inspirational book or a good message on MP3 along with you. Listen to uplifting music or a sermon in the car while driving to work. Take your portable listening device with you when you exercise and listen to some worship music or a good sermon. Use these moments to help fill up your 'Kingdom Life tank'.

- Never turn on your phone, tablet or computer as soon as you wake up in the morning. If you do, you allow others to govern your agenda and your mood. You will be pulled in every which way except your own, getting you off to a chaotic start of your day. Certainly you can do without that chaos in your mind!

- Turn off your phone, tablet or computer when you want to do anything that's important to you. In no way feel obligated to entertain or listen to others at the time of their choosing. Never allow others to barge in on your agenda and determine your direction for the day.

- Always plan your upcoming week on Sunday. Then list and prioritize your activities for the day when you wake up in the morning. Highlight the three most important tasks you want to accomplish that day. Be sure and get those done, no matter what! It will give you a sense of accomplishment and boost your self-confidence.

- Avoid reading, watching, or listening to programs with negative or violent content right before going to bed at night. Your subconscious mind tends to easily absorb and amplify your 'right-before-bed' experiences. This can lead to restlessness and may keep you from having a good night's rest. Let what you focus on during those evening and nighttime hours be positive and uplifting.

- Live outside your comfort zone. Do something you've never done before (something good and meaningful, that is). Speak to that person you've always wanted to approach. Go get that driver's license you've been wanting for so long. Get past your reasoning, get past your feelings. Resolve to LIVE LIFE!

- Last but certainly not least: Whatever you do, after reading this book, never waste time fighting the devil. That could be the single greatest time waster of all. The devil has absolutely no power, except that which you give him by believing in his lies. *Jesus says that the devil is a liar and the father of lies and that there is no truth in him* (John 8:44). He has already been defeated at the cross of Calvary. When the devil whispers his lies into your ears, play the 'Ignore

Game'. He will try to make you believe things about yourself, your circumstances, and your purpose that are not in accordance with the Kingdom of Heaven. When he does, do not rant and rave at him. Turn to your Heavenly Father and begin thanking Him that the opposite of what the devil is trying to make you believe is true. Base everything you say on God's promises about who you are, what you have, and what you can do.

Make it very practical. For example: If the devil tells you that you will never make it, ignore him and instead say: 'Father, I thank *you that you have made me more than a conqueror* (Rom. 8:37), that I'm called to win in life and that *all things are possible for me, because I believe* (Mark 9:23). I thank you for giving me *the desires of my heart* (Ps. 37:4), and my desire is to come through this situation or circumstance victoriously. Get it? That's the Ignore Game in action!

What do you think will happen once the devil notices that instead of making you frustrated, he's driving you straight into the arms of your Heavenly Father? Surely, THAT was not his intention! I assure you that he will ultimately flee from you because you are submitting to God and resisting him. *Submit yourselves, then, to God. Resist the devil, and he will flee from you* (Jas. 4:7). Let's be wise and not waste time fighting battles that have already been won. Agreed?

We have now reached the last part of this chapter. Here I will show you the use of visualization aids. You will learn to make your identity in Christ very tangible to your five senses, and to develop a powerful and easy-to-access meditation tool for your daily use. This section will solidify and bring together every aspect of your identity that we have discussed throughout the pages of this book.

I base the use of my visualization aids on the following three passages from God's Word: Habakkuk 2:2-4 about writing your vision and making it plain, Genesis 30:25-43 about producing in your life what you focus your attention on, and 2 Corinthians 3:18 about being transformed into the same image of the glory of God by beholding Him. Please take time to read these Bible passages for yourself.

Before getting into the practical use of the visualization aids, I want you to note these following points:

- Any visualization aid you create is to reinforce on paper (or, in this case on a poster board) that which you already know to be true in your heart. The vision board is an expression of your identity (who you are, what you have, and what you can do) according to the Kingdom of Heaven. You create your visual aid either with words, pictures, or a combination of the two.

- When using a whiteboard or a cork board separately write each vision on a sticky note or index card and attach it to the board. Once your vision comes alive in the natural world, you remove that particular note or index card and thank God for His abundant provision.

- When you use words to describe your vision, always let them be **positive, first person and present tense**. You can see this in practice in the examples below. Writing it in this way makes it easier for your heart to actually receive it as your current reality, moving you to become excited about who you are in terms of your character, your purpose, and your abilities in Christ.[22]

- Read over, look at, and meditate on your vision (whether written or in pictures) as often as you can. See yourself actually living in the truth of whatever you are visualizing. What does it look like, feel like, sound like, taste like, or even smell like?

The visual aids I refer to can be broken down into three sections: character boards, vision boards, and purpose boards. While all three intend to reveal the totality of your identity in Christ, they can be distinguished by the following:

1. Your personal **character board** presents a clear image of **who you are**. Here you place pictures and/or words depicting things like: I am healthy; I am at my ideal weight; I am cancer free; I am kind; I am loving; I am prosperous; etc.

2. Your personal **vision board** presents a clear image of **what you have**. Here you place pictures and/or words depicting things like: I own my own home; I have a nice car; I have more than enough financial provision; I have a healthy and loving family; etc.

3. Your personal **purpose board** gives a clear image of **what you can do**. Here you place pictures and/or words depicting things like: I use my coaching skills to help people reach their destiny in life; I use my talents in sports to positively influence kids on the street; I use my finances to help single moms purchase food for their families; etc.

Did you notice how just reading the above personal statements, even though they are not even yours, make something come alive on the inside of you? Why? Because visualization paints a real life picture of your identity. It brings out into the natural realm that for which you were specifically created. What you see and read is who the Heavens have already called you to be since the beginning of time. It's what sin and the devil tried to cover up and never wanted you to know about, but now you know! You were created for limitlessress. Isn't that awesome news?

Visualizing your identity has the potential to create that force that pushes you into your God-given destiny. It's like effortlessly crossing a bridge. You get to the other side without hardly realizing it because the steps have become so natural to you. Visualization also helps you easily lay aside all distractions that try to prevent you from being who you already are in Christ. This is the power of using the vision boards as a guide for your life.

Traditionally, a visualization aid displays all three of the aforementioned components of your identity on one single board. Nevertheless, regardless of how you choose to use the board, it will help you maintain a clear vision and create substance for the life that you already have in God.

My favorite way to create the vision board is to use a combination of pictures and words on a large poster board. I first begin by placing a good size picture of myself in the middle of the board. Then, I either print images from the Internet or cut out pictures from magazines, consisting of things that I envision for myself. I then stick them all around my personal picture. The vision immediately comes alive and makes me easily see myself having that for which I am believing God! I then describe my vision in writing under each image, as always positive, first person, and present tense.

One of the visuals I have on my vision board is a picture of the globe. Underneath it I wrote: "My 'How To Thrive' message goes around the world and touches the lives of millions of people". Another visual includes myself together with my husband and kids. Underneath that are the words: "I am a caring mother to my children and a loving wife to my husband."

Additionally, although I have referred to attaching your visual to a board of some kind, please note that your visualization aid can also be copied on an A4 sheet of paper that you can fold and carry with you wherever you go. It can then also be easily referenced during your quiet times of prayer and meditation. Whatever format you choose, get your arts and crafts utensils out and begin creating your vision today!

Focus points and tips for success on my journey to personal thriving, the Kingdom Way:

- I consciously and rigorously eliminate time-wasters from my life and use my time as wisely as I know how.
- I use my vision board to see my true identity come alive and to bring me closer to who I am simply by beholding and believing.

Practical reflection and consideration ('My Lifestyle'): The Word of God says that you are more than a conqueror, and that Jesus has already defeated the devil on your behalf. In what areas are you still fighting the devil? How will you do this differently from now on, and what is your arsenal of verses that you will use? What is one time-waster that you can eliminate from your day?

By doing this exercise I learned about myself that:

_____

_____

_____

_____

_____

_____

_____

_____

_____

_____

_____

_____

_____

SUMMARY AND CONCLUSION

So, there you have it! My account of the five areas you can adjust or radically change in order to thrive, the Kingdom Way! I invite you to take hold of the simple principles presented in this book. They will help you soar above heights you've never before expected to surpass. Not because I say so, but because God does. He has given us everything we need for life and Godliness. Thanks be to Christ's finished work at the cross and the shedding of His blood!

Applying what you've learned in this book will bring into the natural realm that which has already been freely given to you in the spiritual realm. Your life will be absolutely transformed! I encourage you not to be a passive reader of this book, but rather take action and go after all that has been laid aside especially for you.

Do not come to the end of your life not having lived it fully. Be sure you don't get to Heaven only then to discover all that was once available to you here on earth. You have the opportunity to live the life of the Kingdom of Heaven, right here, right now, today! The choice is entirely up to you!

Having said this, I realize that any form of change or adjustment may seem overwhelming at first, especially if many of the truths you read in this book are new to you. It may be hard to take the first step. Still, I encourage you to make a commitment to doing just that: Take that first step!

At the beginning of this book I asked you to choose one

specific area in your life that you want to change. I asked you to walk through the chapters of this book with me, applying the relevant principles as you go. Did you do it? Did you go through the focus points and practical reflection exercises? Did you meditate? Did you take time to go through the process of forgiveness that I presented to you? Please realize that my tone of voice here is not at all one of condemnation. I want to help you to improve your life, but progress can only happen by doing, failing, falling, getting up, and doing it all over again. This is the way to master any habit or negative experience that you want to see altered in your life.

I believe I've done a thorough job in giving you the tools needed to complete this Kingdom Life journey with success. In 'My Truth' you learned to recognize the destructive ways of the kingdom of this world. I instructed you on how to step over into the blessing-filled Kingdom of Heaven by way of repentance. I ended that section with the story of Jesus Christ, the One and Only. I showed you how only He was able to bring you back into fellowship with God - back to who you were created to be - by becoming the ultimate sacrifice.

In 'My Faith' you learned the true meaning of faith and how it is the absolute key to 'let[ting] it be on earth as it is in heaven'. You also received some hands-on meditation exercises to help solidify in your heart the Truth of the Kingdom of Heaven.

In 'My Identity' I showed you your true identity in Christ and how forgiveness frees you from skewed beliefs. You also learned how to stop actions of self-sabotage and take hold of the opportunities life offers you.

In 'My Purpose' I illustrated how to obtain God's provision for you by giving to the Kingdom of Heaven what little you have in this earthly existence. You saw how financial freedom enables you to focus on the pursuit of your God-given purpose. I then gave you some practical tools to begin discovering and living your purpose.

Finally in 'My Lifestyle', I showed you how you could take personal responsibility for living a life worthy of the Kingdom to which you belong. You also learned how to eliminate time-wasters and create your personal visualization aids. You were able to immediately envision yourself being, having, and doing all that God has prepared for you before the beginning of time.

I have done my utmost to lay out for you the Kingdom Way to thrive and not just survive in your personal life. I encourage you to read through this book several times, or as many times as needed. Use it as your practical guide to get God's best into, and out of, your life. But, whatever you do, don't be overwhelmed. Also, don't ever believe that God's acceptance is based on your "arrival". Remember that you are already fully loved and fully accepted by Him. Live your life based on this absolute truth.

On this journey of life, sometimes we experience more victory in one area than in another. That is completely okay. The key is to first keep reminding yourself of how deeply loved you are by God. Then continue to pursue all that you are, have, and can do in Him. Remember that every blessing Christ died to give you is an expression of God's immense love for you. Freely go after all that has been given to you! Do not reject any of it!

I am confident that just reading this book has expanded your capacity for seeing yourself in a new light in God's Kingdom. How you choose to apply what you've learned is entirely up to you. But please, do apply!

Remember, the Kingdom Way will always produce Kingdom results in your life and I guarantee that even the smallest victory will empower you to progressively commit to this process of thriving according to the Kingdom of Heaven! Life will not always be easy. Therefore, be deliberate in applauding and celebrating your victories on this journey as you steadily seek to thrive and not just survive, the Kingdom Way!

ACKNOWLEDGMENTS

I am deeply grateful to everyone who, in one way or another, has contributed to this book becoming a reality:

My husband Richard, who as always encourages and motivates me to get my voice out there and be all that God has called me to be.

My mom and dad, who have believed and continue to believe in me and support me in all my endeavors.

My friends who have read my manuscript and encouraged me to "Please publish this work because the world needs to hear this message".

My family who have not read my manuscript, yet keep encouraging me to share the message that God has placed in my heart.

My life coach Joseph Peck, who made me believe that with God I could achieve all that He intends for me. I also thank him for reading my manuscript and making valuable suggestions for improving my book.

And finally, as mentioned in my dedication, all my present day 'heroes of the faith' - Pastor Joseph Prince, Pastor Dan Mohler, Pastor Tullian Tchividjian, Pastor Jim Richards, and Pastor Gary Keesee. You have taught me Kingdom truths that I can now myself live out and joyfully share with all who want to hear and learn.

A heartfelt 'Thank You' to you all!

ABOUT THE AUTHOR

Melanie Kos-Paula was born in Curaçao in 1969. At the age of 18 she moved to the United States where she majored in Human Development and earned her bachelor's degree.

Beginning in 1991, she fulfilled several functions in Curaçao as well as in Holland, among other things giving social skills training to youth, in addition to females in the criminal justice system and providing aid to refugees. She also offered counseling and instructional courses for parents, teachers, and children in an effort to help restore disrupted relationships between them. From 2001 to 2006 she had an advisory function with the Department of Criminal Affairs of the Child Welfare Council in Holland, first in Eindhoven and later in Lelystad.

In May of 2006 Melanie returned to her island of birth, Curaçao, where she and her husband Richard were blessed with two precious children, Serenah (in 2006) and Joshua (in 2007).

The Pentecostal Church played a large role in Melanie's life from a very young age. Yet, it was not until 1999 that her spiritual life really gained meaning and she began to make God an active partner in her daily life.

In February of 2012 she founded The Upper Room Curaçao, a foundation that proposes to share Father God's unconditional love with all mankind. This is accomplished for the most part through feeding projects and spending meaningful time with the less fortunate – drug addicts, alcoholics, and the homeless.

The Upper Room Curaçao facility also serves as a training center and meditation oasis. It is a place of silence and tranquillity where soft worship music and a candlelight atmosphere help lead visitors (back) to thoughts of faith and meditation on the Word of God.

Melanie is the creator of 'I Thrive in Life'. Her training program 'How to Thrive, Not Just Survive, the Kingdom Way!' teaches people all over the world how to stop struggling to merely get by in life. People learn to live their God-given life with zest and passion, according to the stable and constant principles of the Kingdom of Heaven. She now shares her experiences and best practices through practical training sessions, group and individual coaching programs, seminars, and speeches. Her ultimate aim is to help set people free to walk in their God-given destiny and purpose.

Melanie's first book *My Husband, My Lord, My All* provides a detailed description of her own personal journey of struggle - a journey that ultimately taught her the key principles for thriving instead of merely surviving in life, the Kingdom Way!

In years passed her book has been actively promoted on her island of birth as well as in Holland as she received invitations to speak on several local radio- and television programs, and at Youth- and Women's organizations, Book Clubs, and churches. Melanie has also spoken and sold her books aboard OM Ships International's largest vessel, Logos Hope, on one of their visits to the island of Curaçao.

Meet Melanie and receive her latest blog updates at:
www.melaniekos.com
For information about the activities of The Upper Room Curaçao, go to:
www.melaniekospaula.org

NOTES

1. Kos-Paula, Melanie, *My Husband, My Lord, My All*, Amsterdam: Galilee Media, 2008. Print.

2. *The Holy Bible. King James Version.* Iowa Falls: World Bible Publishers, 1989. Print.

3. *The Holy Bible. New International Version.* Zondervan. Grand Rapids: International Bible Society, 1973, 1978, 1984. Print.

4. Prince, Joseph. *The Power of Right Believing, 7 Keys to Freedom from Fear, Guilt and Addiction.* New York: FaithWords, 2013. Print.

5. Richards, Jim. *Moving Your Invisible Boundaries, Heart Physics: The Key to Limitless Living.* Travelers Rest: True Potential, 2013. Print.

6. You can read the details about my encounter with my husband in my book *My Husband, My Lord, My All.*

7. "Identity." *Oxforddictionaries.com.* Oxford, 2014. Web. 11 August 2014.

8. Reese, Andy. *Freedom Tools for Overcoming Life's Tough Problems*. Grand Rapids: Chosen Books, 2008. Print.

9. You can direct your prayers either to God the Father, Holy Spirit or Jesus, Son of God, depending on what wounds and lies you're dealing with. Remember, this is only a suggestion, so try it and see how it works out for you. If you don't feel comfortable doing it this way, simply direct your prayers to the One in the Godhead you feel most comfortable talking to. God is One, so I'm quite sure that for Him it makes no difference at all.

10. Authority." *Oxforddictionaries.com*. Oxford, 2014. Web. 26 August 2014.

11. "Purpose." *Oxforddictionaries.com*. Oxford, 2014. Web. 26 August 2014.

12. "Principle." *Oxforddictionaries.com*. Oxford, 2014. Web. 30 September 2014.

13. "Law." *Oxforddictionaries.com*. Oxford, 2014. Web. 30 September 2014.

14. McCarthy, Kevin. *The on Purpose Person, Making Your Life Make Sense*. Winter Park: On-Purpose Publishing, 2009. Print.

15. "Lifestyle." *Oxforddictionaries.com*. Oxford, 2014. Web. 16 October 2014.

16. An important side-note here is that we will fall many times throughout our journey of becoming doers of the Word.

Nevertheless it is in those moments of failing that we can turn to the finished work of Christ and thank Him for His forgiveness. It is in those moments that we thank Him that it is His righteousness, not ours, that pulls us through and spurs us on. It is in those moments that we thank Him for not condemning us, because we belong to Him and He to us. Hallelujah, thank You Jesus for such a complete and gracious salvation!

17. "Endurance." *Oxforddictionaries.com.* Oxford, 2014. Web. 1 November 2014.

18. "Integrity." *Oxforddictionaries.com.* Oxford, 2014. Web. 1 November 2014.

19. "Communication." *Oxforddictionaries.com.* Oxford, 2014. Web. 1 November 2014.

20. "Time." *Oxforddictionaries.com.* Oxford, 2014. Web. 3 November 2014.

21. Peck, Joseph. *I Was Busy, Now I'm Not, Changing the Way You Think About Time.* New York: Morgan James Publishing, 2014. Print.

22. In the *'My Purpose'* section of this book I mentioned that you can turn your purpose essay into a visual tool to describe all that God says about you. The way to do this is by converting your purpose essay into positive, first person and present tense statements.